macramé

A Complete Introduction to the Craft of Creative Knotting

By Mary Walker Phillips

Conceived and edited by

William and Shirley Sayles

PAN BOOKS LONDON AND SYDNEY

Foreword

It can be said that we live in a world occupied with the exploration of construction techniques – a world not particularly romantic or introspective. Within the present decade weavers have been increasingly exploring the possibilities of constructing fabrics without the aid of a loom. Exhibitions of contemporary textiles include non-woven fabrics and forms in a variety of techniques. In addition, many of the fabrics used for clothing and furnishing are non-woven, and designers predict that their use will increase in the future. The fact that Mary Walker Phillips began her professional career as a weaver and fabric designer, and is now recognized as our foremost creative knitter, establishes her as a leading force in the current movement to explore non-woven constructions. Her interest in Macramé has been in part the result of her understanding and response to fibres and yarns and her adventure into research and delight in discovery.

Interest in knots has ranged from the intricacies of Leonardo da Vinci's inter-lacings, outlining complex Renaissance theories, to the fanciful fringes and embellishments of the Victorian era. Many cultures, ancient and contemporary, have used knotting as a means of fabric construction or decoration. This includes ritual masks of tribal Africa and fringes on Mexican shawls. Perhaps the most vital heritage, however, has been that of the sailor. Sailors, who have spent their lives with rope, twine, and cord and their interlacings and fastenings, have named countless numbers of knots. They have spent endless hours tying knots as part of their livelihood and as a means of pleasure. Few are aware of the fanciful and creative forms knotted by sailors in their spare time.

Mary Walker Philips is fascinated by the relationship of the uncomplicated process of tying a knot to the clear and direct form of the knot itself. In the process of knotting she ties, re-ties, and constructs to produce an infinite variety of textures and shapes. Not always content with pure form, however, she adds the dimension of function and insists on a high standard of craftsmanship. This book was conceived and written to present clearly outlined projects in Macramé – projects which demonstrate the possibilities of the technique and the variety of functional and non-functional forms which can be created. The emphasis is on the response of the eye and the hand, and, ultimately, the individuality of the craftsman and the unique qualities of his work.

MILTON SONDAY

First British edition published 1972 by Pan Books Ltd.,
Cavaye Place, London SW10 9PG
5th printing 1978
Copyright © 1970 by Western Publishing Company, Inc
ISBN 0 330 23405 6
Printed by Cripplegate Printing Co. Ltd., London and Edenbridge

Contents

ACKNOWLEDGEMENT

Among those who have assisted in the preparation of this book, special thanks are due to:

Remo Cosentino, *Design and Production*

Louis Mervar, *Photography*

Paul Goodfriend Associates, *Diagrams*

Introduction

Sylvia's Book of Macramé Lace, published in England in the 1880s, states that 'Goethe, somewhere or other, in exalting music above every other art, does so on the ground that it produces its marvellous effects with so little display of means and tools; and if this test be applied to our present work, it will rank very high . . . not even a thimble and needle, are wanted to produce the charming effects of our Macramé work.'

Macramé can be practised wherever you are, needing no more space than your lap. The knots themselves are also simple and can be easily followed from the diagrams given in this book.

KNOTS

Only two basic knots are involved – the Half Knot and the Half Hitch – but it is the endless variations on these two knots that generate all the excitement in Macramé. The wonder of this craft is that anything as simple as these two knots can produce such a variety of beautiful things, and such fun in making them. It is no surprise that both those who have become devoted to Macramé and those who are newly initiated find it difficult to leave their knotting boards.

Macramé has been defined as the interknotting of yarns. It is, however, much more than that in terms of the satisfaction that you will discover in the actual process of creating. The work is easier than it seems; a knowledge of knots is all that is necessary to make the most difficult-appearing knotting pattern.

This craft is now in the midst of an enthusiastic revival, and I would like to mention Virginia I. Harvey as one who has made a large contribution to this resurgence of interest. I had already explored this craft before seeing her book, *Macramé: The Art of Creative Knotting*, but, like lots of others, I have benefited greatly from it.

Many of us who had been busy in other crafts are now using this particular medium for several levels of expression – to create works of art, such as the wall hanging shown at left, and to make practical items for the home, such as the projects included in this book. Macramé is for all, for young and old, male and female – for anyone who is attracted by the beauty that exists in simple knots.

A SHORT BACKGROUND

Macramé, like many another craft, suffered a loss of popularity for a time and became almost a lost art. When it was reintroduced towards

A Macramé wall-hanging adds a decorative and exciting touch to what otherwise would be a dull corner

(*Facing page*) Wall-hanging, 'Variations No. 5', 184 mm×445 mm (7$\frac{1}{4}$ in. ×17$\frac{1}{2}$ in.), worked in three colours – in black and white rug wool and brown thread

the end of the Victorian period, people enthusiastically adopted it as a new craft, to such an extent that Sylvia was prompted to write in her book: 'This kind of fancy-work is not exactly a novelty, except in the sense that when anything becomes so old as to be forgotten, its revival has all the effects of a first appearance.' It was put to great use during this period, and elaborate fringes and tassels were produced in enormous quantities to trim curtains, mantelpieces, shelves, and four-poster beds. Sylvia even prompted her 'fair reader . . . to work rich trimmings for black and coloured costumes, both for home wear, garden parties, seaside ramblings, and balls – fairylike adornments for household and underlinen . . .'

The earliest form of Flat Knot work is said to have originated in Arabia during the 13th century – Macramé comes from the Arabic *Migramah*, which means ornamental fringe and braid. The Spaniards, after learning the art from the Moors, spread it to southern Europe, possibly as early as the 14th century – certainly by the 16th, since its use is documented in a painting in Valladolid Cathedral, Spain.

Macramé was also popular in Italy around that time. In more recent days, however, in Turin, at an open-air school called Casa del Sole, young children – some five and six years old – became adept at doing a form of Macramé called the *Cavandoli Stitch*. This stitch, created by Mrs Valentina Cavandoli to amuse and occupy the children in her care, is worked in two colours and is really another name for work produced by Cording. Some Cavandoli work is shown on pages 56–7.

France has produced a great deal of Macramé, and there is sufficient historical data to suggest that it was an established art in that country by the late 14th century. It is not known exactly when *Le Macramé*, by Thérèse de Dillmont, was written, or even when her *Encyclopedia on Needlework*, which contains a chapter on Macramé, was published, but I would venture to say that it was in the early 1800s. The examples in these books are extremely interesting and clearly exhibit the tremendous range of knotting possibilities.

Not to be overlooked is the contribution that seafaring men have made to Macramé. It cannot be said when they first began knotting to while away their long hours at sea, but as early as the 15th century they were using knotted articles for barter in India and China. Outstanding examples of sailors' work are to be found in the many maritime museums.

Macramé is thought to have been introduced into England in the late 1600s by Queen Mary, wife of William of Orange, who learned the craft in Holland. During the time of George III, the knotting of fringes was a great pastime; his wife, Queen Charlotte, in the 1780s was making Macramé fringe at court.

A charming example of Cavandoli work can be seen at the top of this Italian bag with Macramé fringe. Author's collection, gift from Donnie Mac Nab Brown

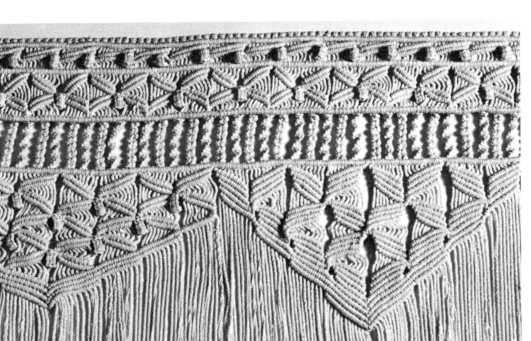

(*Above*) American turn-of-the-century Macramé fringe for four-poster bed, approximately 457 mm (18 in.) high. Collection of Cooper-Hewitt Museum of Design, Smithsonian Institute, Washington, D.C.

(*Right*) American turn-of-the-century Macramé bag made of cotton cord, approximately 356 mm (14 in.) high with fringe. Collection of Elizabeth T. Page

PROJECTS

Since there are so many items that can be knotted, and such a variety of knots to work them in, it might be difficult for the beginner to know where to start. I have therefore presented a cross-section of items from the practical to the decorative. Seventeen projects are included, with complete directions and diagrams wherever necessary. In all instances, a handsome piece can be developed that will give pleasure in the making and in the using as well.

The intention of this book in giving directions is to build confidence so that each idea will be a springboard to your own creativity. Perhaps, after doing a few projects, you will want to try your own ideas, or perhaps you will want to vary a project by adding a knotting variation. By all means do so, and to aid you in this there is information on yarn, colour, design, and texture. This information, together with the knowledge you will have gained from the explanatory text and the diagrams of the knots, should enable you to start on the road to designing your own pieces.

SAMPLERS

Making samples of each knot, and in all its variations, will pay dividends in the understanding that you will soon have of the knotting process. Eventually, you will be able to tell how a piece of Macramé was knotted by just looking at it.

Until a complete knowledge of the knots is achieved, it is recommended that the beginner make samples in one colour – natural or white – since the knots will then be easier to see. Use as many variations on the knots as you wish. By using three different yarns, even greater interest is added. Experiment to your heart's content and then put what you have learned into a finished piece.

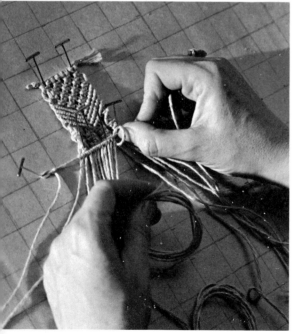

Method of working in Macramé on a knotting board, with the article placed and pinned against guidelines. Here a new cord is being added on with a row of Cording

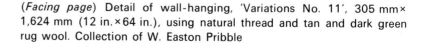

(*Facing page*) Detail of wall-hanging, 'Variations No. 11', 305 mm× 1,624 mm (12 in.×64 in.), using natural thread and tan and dark green rug wool. Collection of W. Easton Pribble

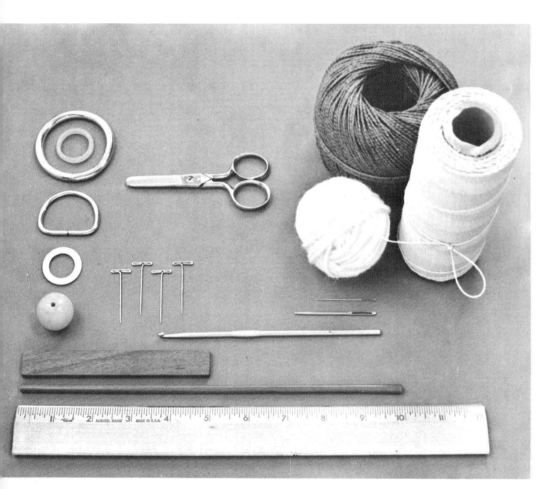

Scissors
Glass-headed Pins
Yarns
Embroidery Needles
Crochet Hook
Woodstrips
Ruler
Beads and Rings
Knotting Board

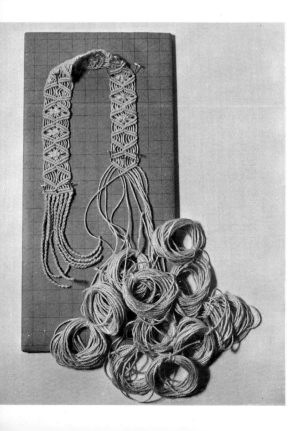

Equipment

The basic tools for Macramé work are simple and consist of scissors, glass-headed pins, and a knotting board. All other items are accessories or adornments. The embroidery needle and crochet hook are used occasionally for finishing off; chopsticks, hardwood, beads, rings, and loops for headings and decorations. Two metal loops make a belt buckle, as shown on pages 50–51.

THE KNOTTING BOARD

The knotting board is the working surface. The most suitable material for this is a piece of insulating board, or cork, covered with brown wrapping paper. The important thing is that the board be lightweight and rigid but soft enough for pins to be inserted easily.

YARNS

Yarns used for Macramé should be strong enough to withstand the abrasion that knotting produces, and should not have a lot of give or elasticity. Smooth-surfaced yarns are best since they are the most satisfactory to work with and do not detract from the textural interest of the knots.

The most widely used yarns are: Macramé twine, Novacord, sisal, jute, crochet cotton, Seine twine, Filler cord, Lurex cord, rug wool and parcel string.

Knitting yarns are not desirable since they have too much elasticity, but some, e.g., Aran wools, can be used once their limitations are understood and samples have been made with them.

The term 'thread' is used throughout the book to mean a yarn other than wool. The illustrations show the relative thicknesses and texture of the yarns. From these readers are encouraged to make their own choice of thread and colours.

Handspun yarns of quality lend themselves well to the more knowledgeable knotter. The Indians of Mitla, Mexico, who work beautifully in Macramé, do a great deal of their knotting in these yarns. Two examples of their work are shown on pages 44–5. Very heavy unspun roving provides scale and is interesting when combined with other yarns, as in Cascade, pages 72–3.

1 Strutts super glacé gimp	**7** Lurex cord
2 Strutts glacé	**8** Piping cord
3 'Needlewoman' Macramé twine	**9** Parcel string
4 Filler cord	**10** Broplene twine
5 Nylon Seine twine	**11** Turkey rug wool
6 Novacord	**12** 4-ply sisal

Project Previews

A few projects that appear in this book are shown on these two pages to introduce you to Macramé pieces that you can make. I have tried to present a varied arrangement throughout to suit different interests, tastes, and developments of skill.

In addition to the many pieces that I made for the projects, I have also presented some of my wall-hangings (an example is on the facing page), and have described them as to technique, knots, and materials used. This analysis was done not so that you could copy the individual pieces, but so that you would be better able to understand the progression of knots in their variations and how their combination can produce a work of art. Rugs and mats, also included as projects, are a relatively new departure for Macramé and one that I hope you will find exciting.

This combination of projects and analysis of technique offers the best way to begin your adventure into Macramé. While the pieces presented are all different, they have one thing in common – they are all made up of the two basic knots (the Half Hitch and the Half Knot) and their variations.

As you build up your skills and become more and more intrigued with the interplay of knotting patterns and yarn textures, new ideas and endless possibilities for further exploration will open up before you.

(*Left*) Hanging vase – see page 31

(*Below*) Belt No. 2 – see pages 50–51

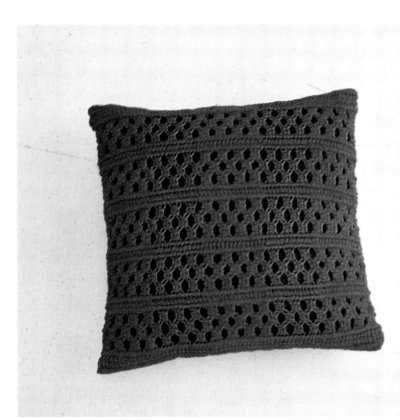

Cushion cover – see pages 42–3

Blue and gold rug – see pages 52–3

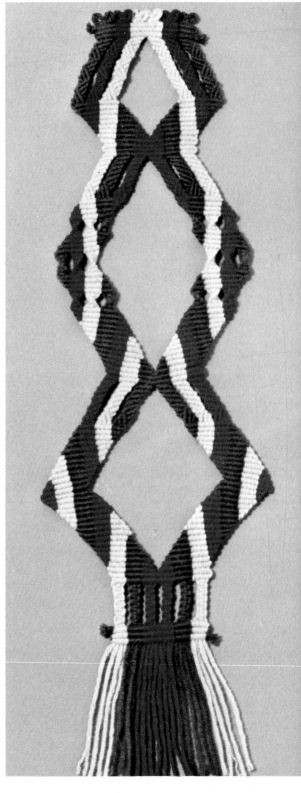

Wall-hanging, Spirit of '76 – see pages 60–61

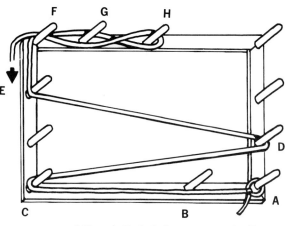

(*Above*) Ends being measured off on a warping board. Note the cross between G and H. (*Below*) Ends can also be measured off on an expanding hat rack

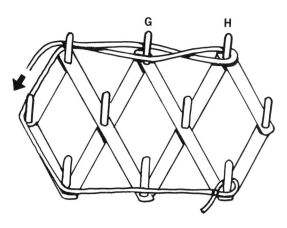

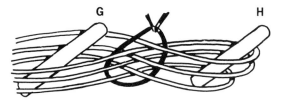

Close-up of cross, showing loose loop of contrasting yarn separating the ends

Preparing the Yarn

The yarn is prepared for knotting by calculating the length of the ends and measuring off. An *end* is an individual length of yarn.

HOW TO CALCULATE

The ends should be $3\frac{1}{2}$ to 4 times longer than the piece you plan to make, but since they are doubled in half for knotting, they are measured 7 to 8 times longer. For example, if the piece will have a finished length of 0·9 m (1 yd), measure each end to 6·4 m or 7·3 m (7 or 8 yd). When each end is doubled for knotting, it will then be two ends, each 3·1 m to 3·6 m ($3\frac{1}{2}$ to 4 yd) long. Measure ends generously and then add to them. This is no time to apply 'Waste not, want not.' It is better to have extra yarn than to run short and have to add at an inconvenient place in the design. If, however, you should be in this situation, see Splicing, page 25.

Making a Sample. Heavy yarns take up more length in knotting than lightweight ones, so allow for this in the calculations. Make a sample, at least 76 mm × 152 mm (3 in. × 6 in.) to gauge the length and to see how many ends will be needed for the width. To determine the number, tie four ends into a Flat Knot (see pages 16–17) and measure the knot's width. If it is 12 mm ($\frac{1}{2}$ in.) for example, you know you will need eight ends to the inch.

When you know what you want to make, or if you are searching for ideas, knot the yarn in several ways to know how it will tie and to gauge its texture and desirability. Keep notes of the amount used, its source, the number of ends and their length. Such records are valuable when planning future Macramé pieces.

MEASURING OFF ENDS

Warping Board. Once you know how long the ends should be, measure them off. This can be done with a 0·5 m × 0·9 m ($\frac{1}{2}$ yd × 1 yd) weaver's warping board. Begin by cutting one end, in a contrasting colour, to the calculated length. Tie this measuring cord around peg A and wind it out to its full length as shown in the diagram. Making a cross between pegs G and H keeps the ends in order. With the measuring cord as guide, measure off the ends and cut them at peg A. In this way, ends may be removed in sections, and measurements will not be lost. To keep easier count of the ends, tie every group of ten with a loose loop of contrasting yarn.

Other Methods. If you don't have a warping board, C-clamps, or holding pegs, can be used. Attach clamps to opposite ends of a table and wind the yarn from peg to peg. Remember to make the cross. There is still another method. It takes longer, but it works. Measure the yarn against a yardstick, then cut it. Keeping this end as the measuring cord, measure off the needed number of ends.

MOUNTING ENDS

Knotting Board. The board is covered with brown wrapping paper, which affords good contrast to the yarns. Pull the paper tightly over the board, tape it on the reverse side, and mark it off into 25 mm (1 in.) squares. These guidelines will help you knot to the correct length and width. Work at the board in the way most comfortable for you – I usually sit with the board leaning against a table edge and resting in my lap. A convenient point to begin the work is usually the middle of the board, or about 254 mm (10 in.) from the bottom. As knotting progresses, move the work upwards.

Holding Cord. The ends are knotted onto a holding cord (a horizontal length) with the Reversed Cording Knot (see diagram; also page 17) or onto a chopstick, ring, bracelet or whatever you feel suits the piece. They can also be looped around the pins.

Tie an Overhand Knot onto each side of the holding cord and pin securely to the knotting board. The cord must be kept taut. At times it is also used as a knot-bearing cord (over which knots are tied); in that case, make an Overhand Knot on one side only, preferably the left.

As each end is knotted onto the holding cord, pin it to the board. Move pins down constantly as the work progresses. They should never be more than 25 mm (1 in.) from the working area and can even be just in the row above. Slant pins away from you, and *anchor them firmly*. If the design should become irregular, either the pinning is not sufficient or some knots are being tied too tightly.

WINDING ENDS

When ends are too long to handle conveniently, their lengths can be reduced by making hand bobbins or butterflies (see diagrams), or by using rubber bands. Each end is wound separately.

KNOTS

Only two elementary knots are essential to Macramé – the Half Knot, also called the Macramé Knot, and the Half Hitch. There are various combinations of these knots, some distinctive enough to have their own names. Different texts refer to them under different names but, once seen, they can be recognized as old friends.

Knots can be easily learned from the diagrams in this book. In addition to those in the section on Knots which follows, others are included in the book where they apply. Practise them by making samples, using different yarns and doubling the number of ends. Make the knots in light-coloured yarns so that they will be easier to see.

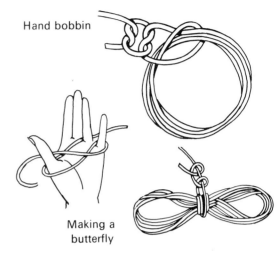

Hand bobbin

Making a butterfly

Hand Bobbin: Wind the ends in circles around the fingers and fasten with a Flat Knot when ends reach about 457 mm (18 in.) from holding cord

Butterfly: Clasp loose end of yarn and wind length in figure 8s as shown

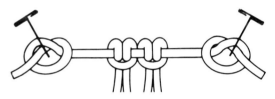

Two Reversed Cording shown mounted on a holding cord. The two Overhand Knots on either side are pinned securely to the knotting board

---

THINGS TO REMEMBER

Keep the holding cord in a steady position when mounting ends.

Keep the knot-bearing cord motionless and taut when in use.

Tie every knot close to the previous knot unless the design directs otherwise.

Keep ends straight, in order, and not twisted, particularly when knots are being made over them.

Ends are always doubled in half before knotting begins. When the number of cut ends is given in the projects, this always refers to measured-off ends and not to doubled ends.

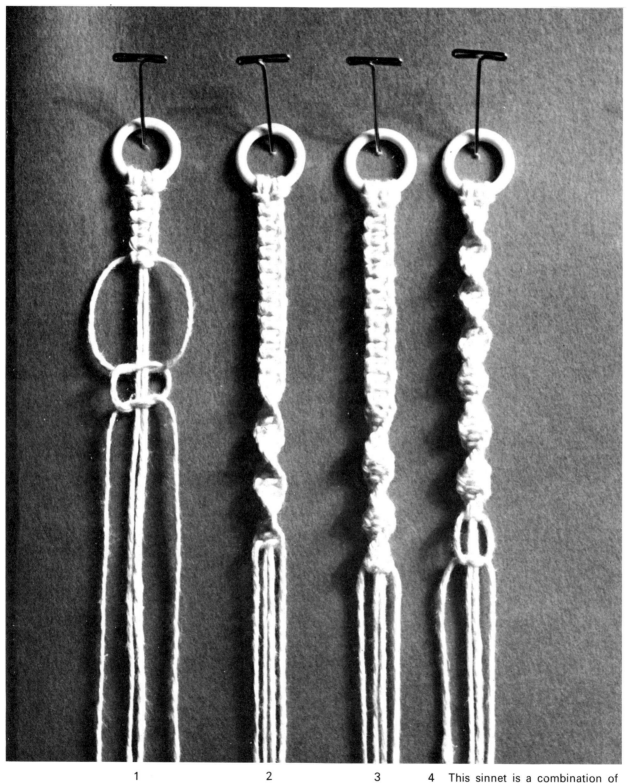

1   2   3   4 This sinnet is a combination of
                                   left-right, right-left Half Knots

The Flat Knot and the Half Knot

The Flat Knot is made up of two Half Knots, one going to the left, the other to the right. Four ends are used; the centre two, known as fillers or core ends, are held taut until the knot is completed. As you practise you will be making sinnets (braided cording) as seen on the facing page. The knotting patterns below correspond by number with those used in the sinnets illustrated. In Sinnet No. 1 the knotting pattern consists of a series of Flat Knots. In Sinnets 2 and 3, using a Flat Knot and a Reversed Flat Knot respectively, a twist effect is obtained in the lower sections by repeating the Half Knot. Sinnet 4 is a combination of the lower sections of Sinnets 2 and 3. In Sinnets 1 and 4 the last knot is shown in construction.

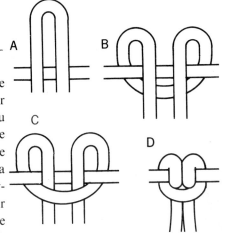

A B C D

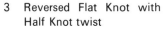

How to mount ends on holding cord with Reversed Cording

TO MAKE SINNETS ON FACING PAGE

1 Flat Knot

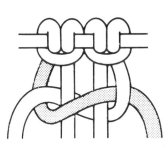

Half Knot, left-right

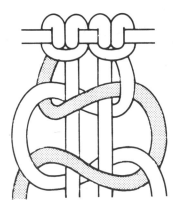

Flat Knot, left-right, right-left, completed. Continue with series of Flat Knots

2 Flat Knot with Half Knot twist

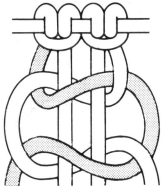

Flat Knot

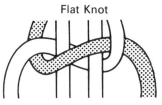

Continue Half Knot, left-right, to make twist

3 Reversed Flat Knot with Half Knot twist

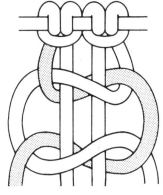

Reversed Flat Knot

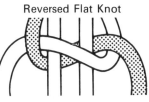

Continue Half Knot, right-left, to make twist

Flat Knot sinnet of leather made into handles adds new interest to old bureau drawers

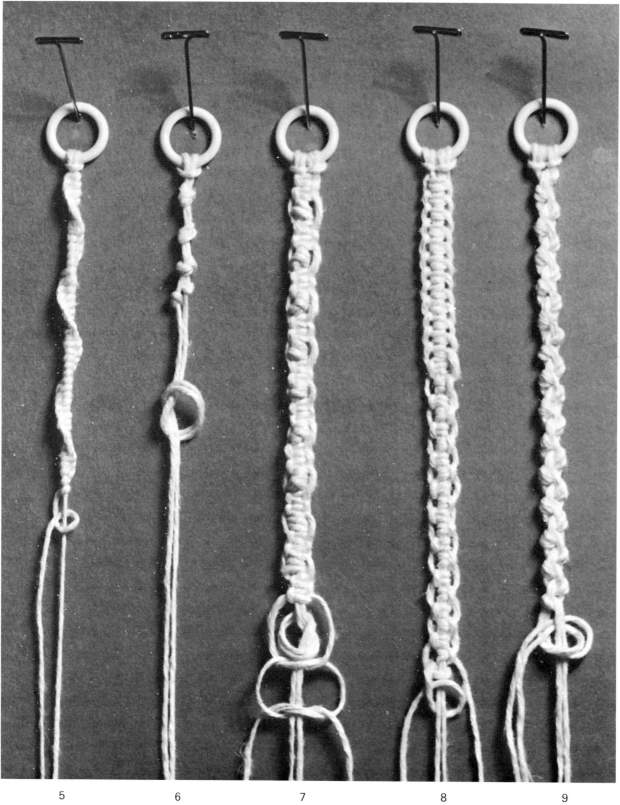

5   6   7   8   9

The Half Hitch, The Overhand Knot

The Half Hitch is the most practical knot in Macramé since a number of variations may be obtained from it. The Overhand Knot is tied in a way somewhat similar to the Half Hitch but is applied differently. A series of Overhand Knots using either a single end or multi-ends creates texture. It also can be used to end a sinnet. In diagram 7, it is used between Flat Knots for added interest.

The Double Chain Knot can be made with two ends or multi-ends. Using it in two colours with a heavy yarn makes an interesting sash.

The construction of all these knots can be easily followed from the diagrams. In each case the knotting patterns correspond by number with those used in the sinnets on the facing page.

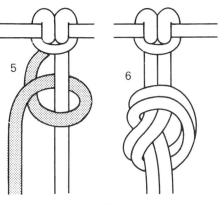

5 Half Hitch Knot
Continue for sinnet

6 Overhand Knot, two ends
Continue for sinnet

TO MAKE SINNETS ON FACING PAGE

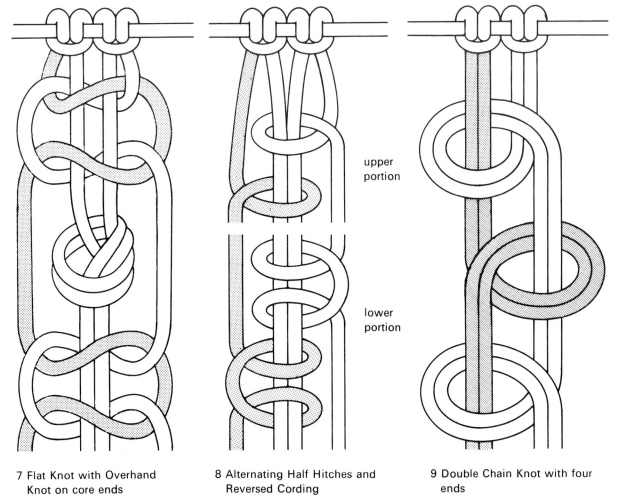

upper portion

lower portion

7 Flat Knot with Overhand Knot on core ends

8 Alternating Half Hitches and Reversed Cording

9 Double Chain Knot with four ends

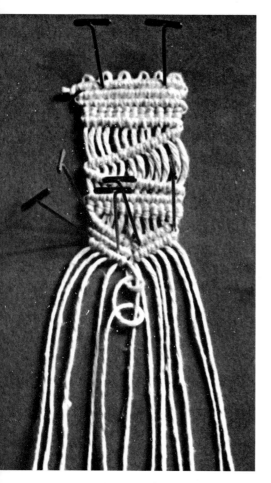

Sampler showing Horizontal, Vertical, and Diagonal Cording

Cording

It would be difficult to say which of the Cording variations gives the most exciting results. They are certainly all distinctive. This book contains several projects that well illustrate the endless possibilities of this important and versatile knot. Three versions are diagrammed here – the Horizontal, Vertical, and Diagonal. Each end goes over the knot-bearing cord twice while completing the row (making two Half Hitches). Keep the knot-bearer secure across each row and held sharply in the determined direction. Draw up knots closely and pin each row after completion. The knot-bearer must be measured off longer than other ends.

TO MAKE HORIZONTAL ROWS

A End 1 is knot-bearer

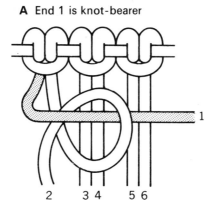

B With end 2, make Cording

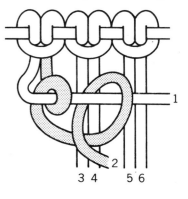

C Repeat for end 3

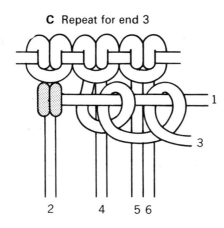

D Complete row and return

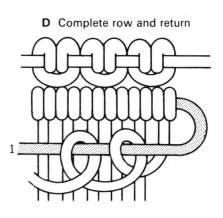

TO MAKE VERTICAL ROWS

A Start

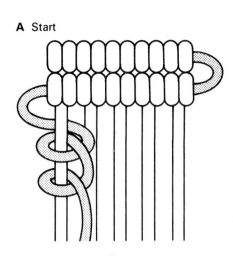

B Continue

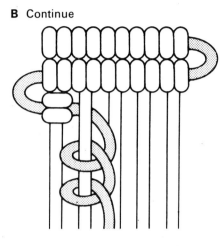

C Return

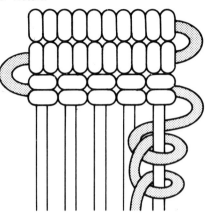

TO MAKE DIAGONAL ROWS

A End 1 is knot-bearer

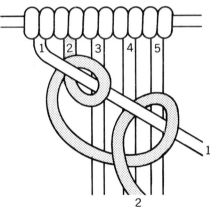

B With each end, make Cording

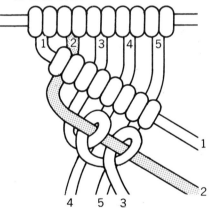

C Start 2nd row with end 2 as knot-bearer

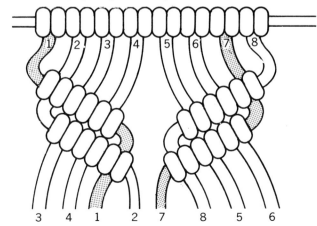

D Method of crossing ends when diagonal rows meet

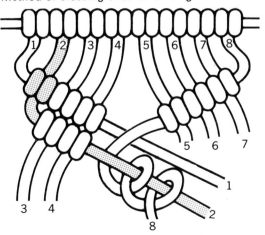

E To create open spaces, diagonal rows are not crossed

Continue by making a row of knots with end 7, then tie it over end 1

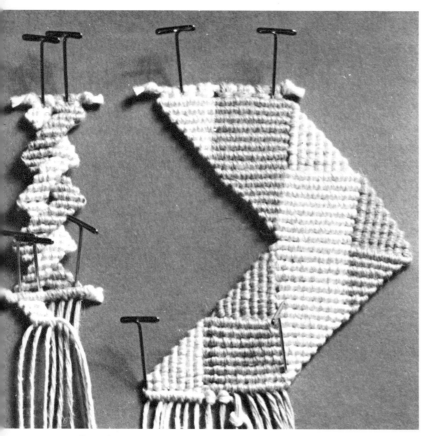

Sample 1   Sample 2

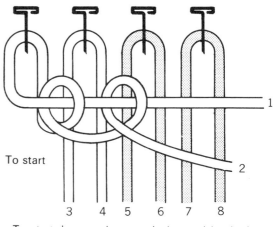

To start

To start, loop ends around pins and begin 1st row of Horizontal Cording

FACING PAGE:

A, B, C Start angling technique, working from left to right.

D To continue, end 5 is brought to horizontal position and Horizontal Cording starts with end 6.

AA To reverse angling pattern direction.

BB To vary colour pattern.

Cording (Angling Technique)

The Horizontal and Vertical Cording can be varied in an angling technique which makes colour changes possible, as well as the creating of pointed areas for profile shaping.

Sample 1 consists of two angled sections made independently with Horizontal Cording. The yarn is knotted from right to left for the first section and then from left to right. This alternating is continued until the desired length is reached. The second section is done in the same way, but the knotting starts from left to right. When both sections are the same length, they are interlocked simply by being placed together and secured with a row of Horizontal Cording on a holding cord.

Sample 2 consists of interknotting of colours by the angling technique. One by one ends are worked across in rows of Horizontal Cording and are left on the right side. After a number of ends have been done, they are brought straight down and are used as knot-bearing cords for Vertical Cording. The diagrams demonstrate the technique used.

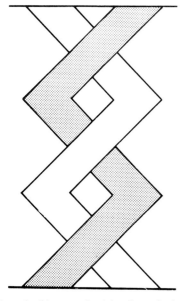

Interlocking method for Sample 1

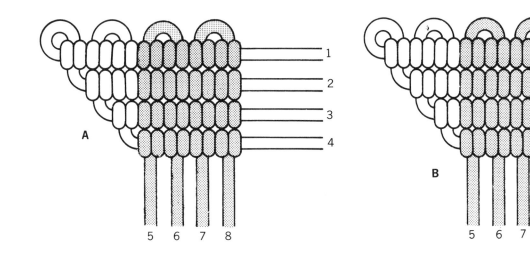

A

1
2
3
4

5 6 7 8

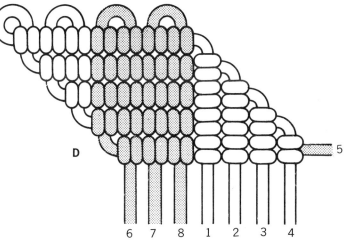

B

3
4

5 6 7 8 1 2

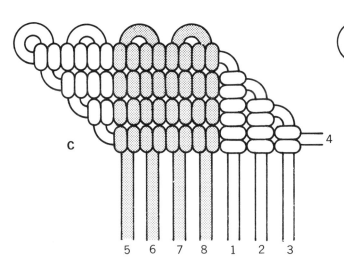

C

4

5 6 7 8 1 2 3

D

5

6 7 8 1 2 3 4

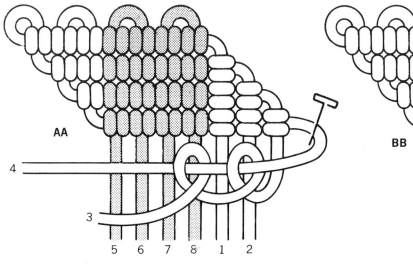

AA

4

3

5 6 7 8 1 2

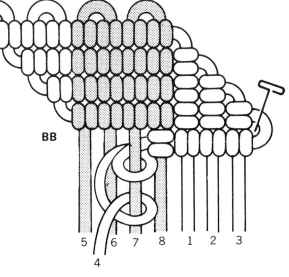

BB

5 6 7 8 1 2 3

4

Headings and Picots

There are various ways of mounting ends onto a holding cord and some are very decorative.

The picots shown here are looped knots used to give variation to edge headings and other areas where a lacy effect is desired. Note the Hanging Vase on page 31.

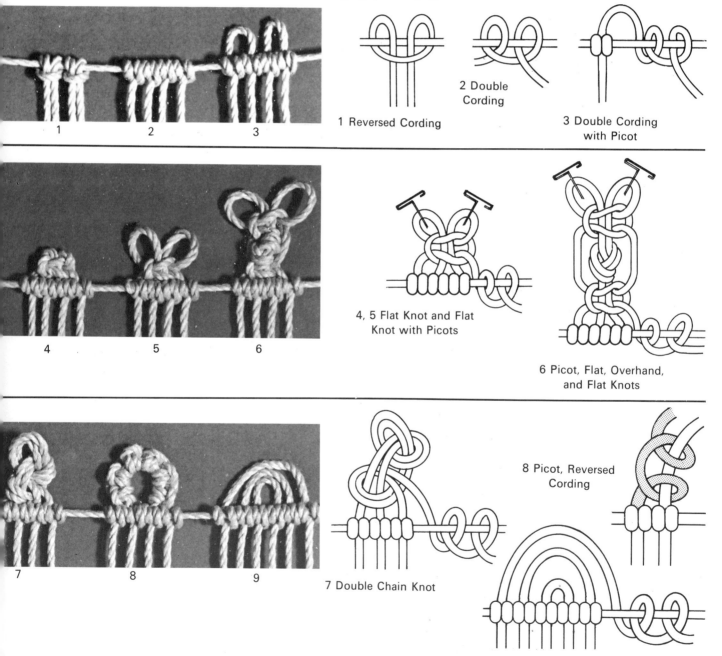

1 Reversed Cording

2 Double Cording

3 Double Cording with Picot

4, 5 Flat Knot and Flat Knot with Picots

6 Picot, Flat, Overhand, and Flat Knots

7 Double Chain Knot

8 Picot, Reversed Cording

9 Series of picots

Finishing

For finishing off a piece, the remaining ends can be worked into a decorative fringe, or formed into sinnets, or they can be neatly trimmed, making a simple fringed edge. A Gathering Knot can be made (see diagram), using as many ends as you want. Tie it tightly so that it will hold and give a crisp look to the work. The ends can also be woven into the reverse side with an embroidery needle or crochet hook. Still another way is to set in a holding cord and mount a single row of Cording, followed by a Flat Knot and sinnets ending with a Gathering Knot. These and other ways of ending pieces will be found in the projects.

Decorative Edgings. Flat Knots with multi-ends and Overhand Knots can be used to make decorative edges on curtains or tablecloths. The same idea can also be added to a sash, or to a knitted stole or blanket.

The curtain fringe in hessian on the right was started by pulling out about 305 mm (12 in.) of the horizontal threads; Flat Knots using twelve ends were then made. The directions are as follows:

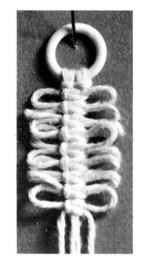

10 Picots with Flat Knots

> 1st row Flat Knot 4,4,4 (4 ends on each side are tied over 4 ends)
> 2nd row – Flat Knot 2,8,2 (2 ends on each side are tied over 8 ends)
> 3rd row – Flat Knot 4,4,4
> 4th row – Flat Knot 2,8,2
> 5th row – Overhand Knot with the centre 8 ends.
> 6th and 7th rows – Flat Knots 2,4,2, using the 8 ends.
> 8th row – Overhand Knot with the centre 8 ends.
> 9th row – Flat Knot 4,4,4
> To Finish: Make a Gathering Knot and trim ends neatly.

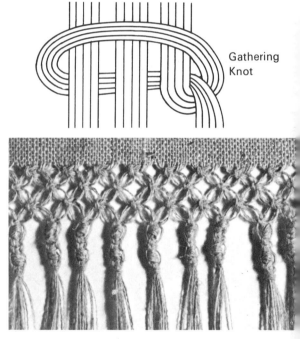

Gathering Knot

Curtain fringe in hessian

splicing

At times ends must be replaced because their lengths were under-estimated or they were pulled so tightly they snapped. In those instances splicing can be done. If the end breaks in a row of Cording, overlap the broken ends and continue knotting the row, working them in (see diagram). Pull the exposed ends to the reverse side of the piece. For splicing at core of Flat Knot, see diagram. When working on a large piece it is better to splice than to work with over large butterflies. (See Blue & Gold rug, pages 52–3.)

switching ends

If you find on beginning a Flat Knot sinnet, that the outside ends are much shorter than the core ends, switch them so that the core ends are on the outside. In this way you will not have to splice.

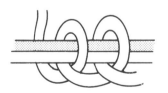

Splicing method for Cording

Splicing method for Flat Knot

Texture

The beauty of a Macramé piece is contained in the movement of the knots. The way they are arranged in a knotting pattern and the yarns that are chosen to work them combine to create a wealth of textural variations. Here are some examples, including several taken from pieces in this book.

COMBINING TEXTURES

The wall-hanging to the left illustrates how a variety of materials can be harmoniously blended to create a unity in design and a richness of texture. A silver metal earring for mounting the work, wooden beads set in among knots, bobbles (see page 49) for raised areas, and two types of yarns in muted colours are all carefully balanced in a construction containing solid areas and open spaces. Added to these elements are the knotting patterns of the Cording and Flat Knot, which give direction and increased interest to the work.

OPEN SPACES WITH LINEAR KNOTTING DESIGN

On the upper right is a detail of a Mexican stole. The emphasis in this piece is on the unevenness of the handspun wool yarn that was used, and the way in which the unknotted areas seem to be loosely held together by a linear pattern of Half Knots. The open textural effect is that of an airy fabric, soft and pliable to the touch, yet it has bulk and is actually very sturdy. It is an ideal apparel texture.

CLOSE KNOTTING WITH RUG WOOL YARN

The detail in the centre of a blue and gold rug is an example of how compactness in design can create texture. This strong, even-surfaced fabric was achieved by close knotting of the Cording worked horizontally and vertically. Rug yarn is used throughout to produce a thick pile and the firmness necessary for its intended use.

COMBINING CONTRASTING YARNS

The detail at lower right of the wall-hanging Cascade exhibits yet another textural quality. This one shows the distinctly different effect achieved when contrasting yarns are combined. Here unspun thick wool and thread are used. The result of their constant interplay becomes the dominant feature in this work, created mainly with the Flat Knot.

(Facing Page) Detail of wall-hanging, Misterio, shows a variety of materials combined. Collection of Anne Stackhouse

Detail of Mexican stole—see also pages 44–5

Detail of blue and gold rug—see also pages 52–3

Detail of wall-hanging, Cascade—see also pages 72–3

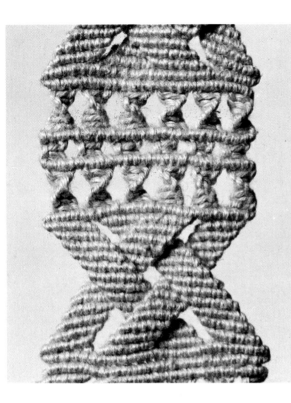

(*Top*) Detail of wall-hanging, Peking—see also pages 64–5

(*Right*) Detail of multicolour sash—see also pages 48–9

(*Below*) Detail of back of red cushion cover—see also pages 42–3

Colour and Design

Although colour is so personal to each of us and our own reactions to it vary as do our moods, there are nevertheless several colour considerations to keep in mind when planning a piece of Macramé. Remember that the beauty of this craft is in its knotting and the way it is arranged in patterns. However, if you have an interesting design in mind, and you want to use colour, or if you desire a particular colour accent in a room, by all means plan the Macramé piece in the colour or colours of your choosing; but it would then be best to keep the construction of the knotting simple.

One way to test what happens to colour in a design is to make samples using different-textured materials and a variety of knots.

INTRICATE PATTERN, USING ONE COLOUR

When a piece is planned to combine different textures, an intricate knotting pattern, and added elements of design, colour is best used singly. Note the detail of Peking (*facing page, top left*), in which some of the knotting variations can be seen. The colour matches and blends with the beads that are incorporated as part of the design. The sparkle of the beads and their colour variations need no further colour contrast to offset them.

TWO YARNS OF THE SAME COLOUR

Using closely related values of one colour can give more interest and depth to the finished piece. The detail of the red cushion (*facing page, lower left*) is an example of how two different yarns of the same colour can work to enhance each other. The elegant sheen of the red rayon is well complemented by the quiet mat finish of the red wool. Another dimension of contrast is added where two yarns meet in areas of Flat Knots. The knotting pattern is kept simple.

STRONG COLOUR CONTRAST

In the detail of the sash (*facing page, right*), multicolour ends of two different yarns are knotted into a repeat diagonal design. Three dramatic colours can be successfully combined because the knotting pattern is a subtle one. The piece is worked periodically from the back, thus changing the character of the surface and contributing an added textural element. Bobbles are another design interest.

ONE COLOUR WITH CONTRASTING BEADS

Colour contrast is also achieved by varying the density of the knotted areas. The detail of Nightbird (*right*) shows a knotting pattern sufficiently interesting to require only white wooden beads for contrast. These beads serve to unify the open spaces and dense areas in the pattern. They also accent the outline of the triangular shape.

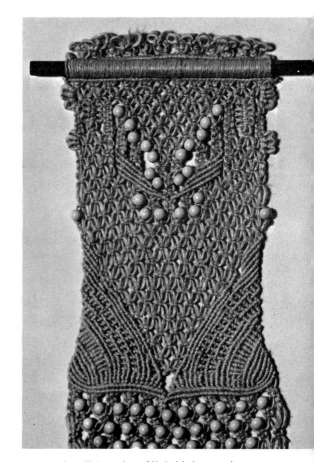

Detail of wall-hanging, Nightbird–see also pages 74–5

Hanging pot plant holder made with Double Chain Knot sinnets

Hanging Pot Plant Holders

The three projects shown here use sinnets and few knots. They are designed to help you create charming and useful pieces by combining yarn and found objects. *Note*: the general rule that ends should measure $3\frac{1}{2}$ to 4 times the finished length of the piece does not apply to the holder for dried grasses or hanging vase. Since there are so few knots to tie in these pieces less yarn is taken up.

Remember, ends are always doubled before knotting begins.

hanging pot plant holder

Size: 508 mm (20 in.).
Materials: Natural thread.
Knot: Double Chain (use 4 ends as 2 – see pages 18–19).
Cut Ends: 2 ends, each 5·9 m (6½ yd) long. 4 ends, each 4·3 m (4¾ yd) long.
Directions: Pin the two 5·9 m (6½ yd) – long ends to the board, leaving a small loop at the top. Tie a sinnet of Double Chain Knots. Attach finished sinnet around container by pulling the ends through the loop.

Mount the remaining found ends onto the finished sinnet at intervals of one-third. Make two Double Chain Knot sinnets where you have attached the ends.
To Finish: Tie the three sinnets together with an Overhead Knot. Trim excess as desired.

holder for dried grasses

Materials: Twine. Any cylindrical- or conical-shaped container. A disc with four holes or a ring is used for the base.
Knots: Flat, Reversed Cording, Overhand.
Cut Ends: 8 ends, each 2·4 m (2¾ yd) long.
Directions: See facing page.
To Finish: Tie the ends together with an Overhand Knot and trim.

hanging vase

Materials: Twine. The container is a triangular jam jar.
Knots: Flat, Overhand, Picot.
Cut Ends: 6 ends, each 2·7 (3 yd) long.
Directions: See facing page.
To Finish: About 711 mm (28 in.) from the last knot, gather the ends together and make an Overhand Knot by which to hang the piece.

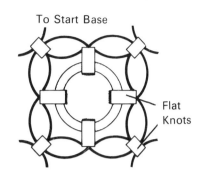

To Start Base

Flat Knots

Directions, dried grasses holder.
Into each hole of the base, or at four
places on a ring, mount two ends,
using the Reversed Cording. This
gives four ends from each hole. Make a
Flat Knot with each four ends. Take
two ends from each knot; leave 32 mm
(1¼ in.) space. Tie a Flat Knot, Overhand Knot, and Flat Knot. Take two
ends from each knot; leave 50 mm
(2 in.) space. With outside ends of
each Flat Knot, tie an Overhand Knot
with four ends.

To Start Base

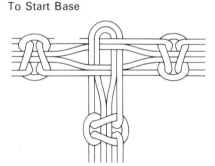

Directions, Hanging Vase. Inter-
twine four ends with the loop ends.
With each four ends, make a sinnet of
5 Flat Knots. *Take the two outside
ends and leave 25 mm (1 in.) space.
Make an Overhand Knot. Bring one
core end each from 2 Square Knots
and make a Flat Knot below the Overhand Knot. Next make 3 Picot Knots
(page 24), ending with 1 Flat Knot *.
Repeat * to * with the other ends. Take
two ends from each knot, leave
50 mm (2 in.) space, and tie an Overhand Knot with four ends. Do 2 more
such knots with the other ends.

Holder for dried grasses with Flat Knots
alternating. Pottery by Charlie Brown

Hanging vase with picots

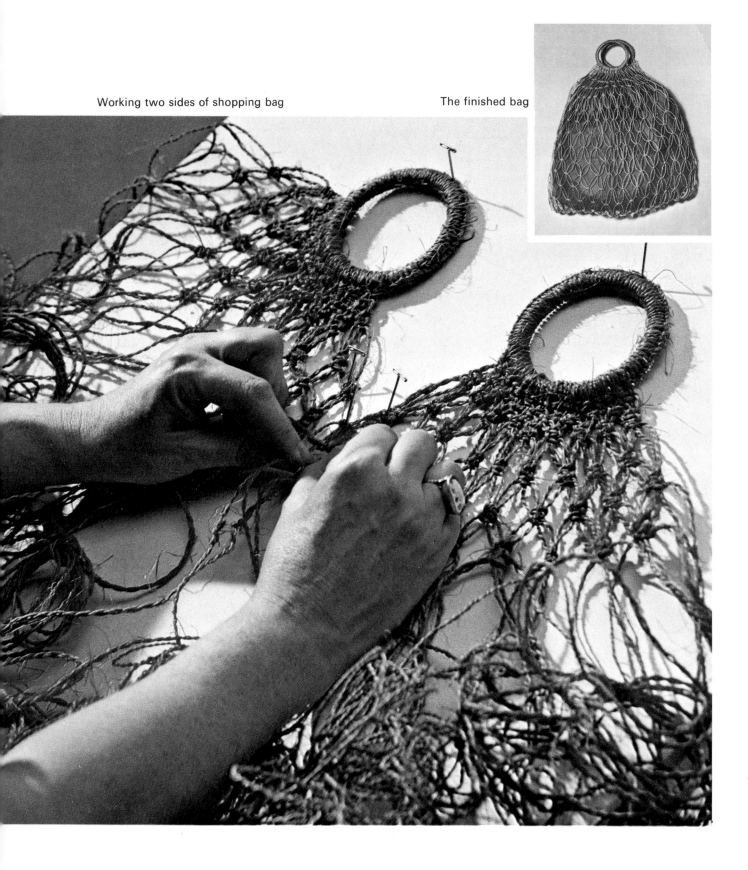

Working two sides of shopping bag

The finished bag

Shopping Bag

This project results in a handy and attractive piece and serves to introduce the Flat Knot used double and in an alternating technique. It is important here that the knots be kept evenly spaced.

Size: 380 mm (15 in.) wide at the centre, 610 mm (25 in.) long, including bracelets and fringe.

Materials: Pink and green thread. This tying cord is available where gift wrappings are sold.
Two bracelets. If you can get matching coloured bracelets, do so; then they will not have to be covered with knots.

Knots: Half Hitch, Reversed Cording, Flat and Double Flat in alternating rows.

Cut Ends: Pink – 18 ends, each 3·66 m (4 yd) long. Green – 18 ends, each 3·66 m (4 yd) long. 2 extra ends, one of each colour, 0·9 m (1 yd) long each, to cover bracelets.

Note: Use a long narrow knotting board since it will be inserted between the two sides of the piece. As you make each knot, dampen it with wet fingertips. Do not get knots too wet or the yarn fibres will separate.

To Begin: Partially cover one bracelet with pink yarn, using the Half Hitch. Attach 10 ends (that is, 5 doubled) of pink with the Reversed Cording. Attach 16 ends (8 doubled) of green in the same manner. Attach 10 more ends of pink in the same manner. Fill up remaining spaces with Half Hitches in pink. Repeat with second bracelet except reverse the colour order.

Directions: Work each side as follows: 2 rows Flat Knots alternating. Knot them close together. 1 row of Double Flat Knots alternating (*see lower diagram*). Leave 10 mm (¾ in.) space and do a 2nd row of Double Flat Knots alternating. Leave 25 mm (1 in.) space and do a 3rd row of Double Flat Knots alternating.

Pin the two sides next to each other and on each side do 3 more rows of Double Flat Knots alternating.

Now join the sides together as shown in the photograph, using the edge of the knotting board. From this point on the piece lies on both sides of the board. Continue knotting to the length of the bag.

To Finish: When you have worked all the knots down to the same point, match the two sides knot for knot. Tie bundles of 8 ends together, using an Overhand Knot and leave 50 mm (2 in.) hanging. Or turn the bag inside out, tie an Overhand Knot on the inside, and trim excess close to the knot.

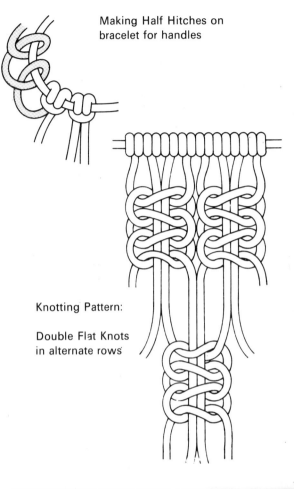

Making Half Hitches on bracelet for handles

Knotting Pattern:

Double Flat Knots in alternate rows

Joining the two sides on edge of knotting board

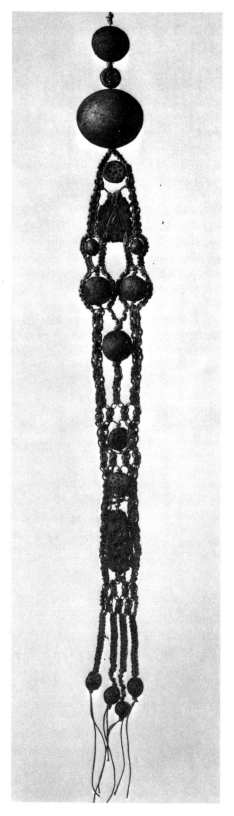

Patio Hangings

Simple sinnets move into a new dimension when they are used in multiples, and there is increased textural interest when they are combined with other materials.

The two hanging pieces shown on this and on the facing page combine Macramé with raku pottery pieces, and are examples of how one craftsman's work can enhance and support another's.

Charlie Brown, a well-known potter in America, from Florida, had sent me an assortment of raku beads, balls and discs to incorporate with Macramé. The considerations in planning these pieces were proper balance and distribution of the raku, always keeping in mind the textural quality of their surface enrichment and the difference in their sizes. A heavy yarn was called for, a dark-coloured one, to complement the smoky shadings of the fired pieces. Twine was used both for its texture and colour and for its durability.

There were certain limitations to be faced in planning the designs due to the uneven distribution of the raku pieces I had available. For the patio hanging on the facing page, I selected nine beads of one size, seven beads of another, three lozenge-shaped beads, one odd bead, and one disc.

The layout of the beads indicated using an odd number of them across the top and then working several rows before adding two beads in the centre with the disc placed evenly beneath them. From this point on, the working areas were divided into three parts, using the remaining beads in the manner shown. The piece is composed of sinnets made up primarily of three knots – Flat, Overhand, and Reversed Half Hitch.

The second piece (*left*) although similarly planned, was not made as a wall-hanging but as a free-hanging suspended form.

Once again with an odd number of raku pieces, I built a design. The largest two of the beads were chosen to head the piece, with a small flat disc placed between them, and the knotting began from this point. Additional ends of twine were added on in several places in order to develop the width dictated by the placement of the beads. This piece was made up of simple sinnets using Flat Knots and Overhand Knots.

(*Left and facing page*) Multi-sinnets combined with raku beads and discs were used to make these two patio hangings. Collection of Signature Shop, Atlanta, Georgia. Raku pieces by Charlie Brown

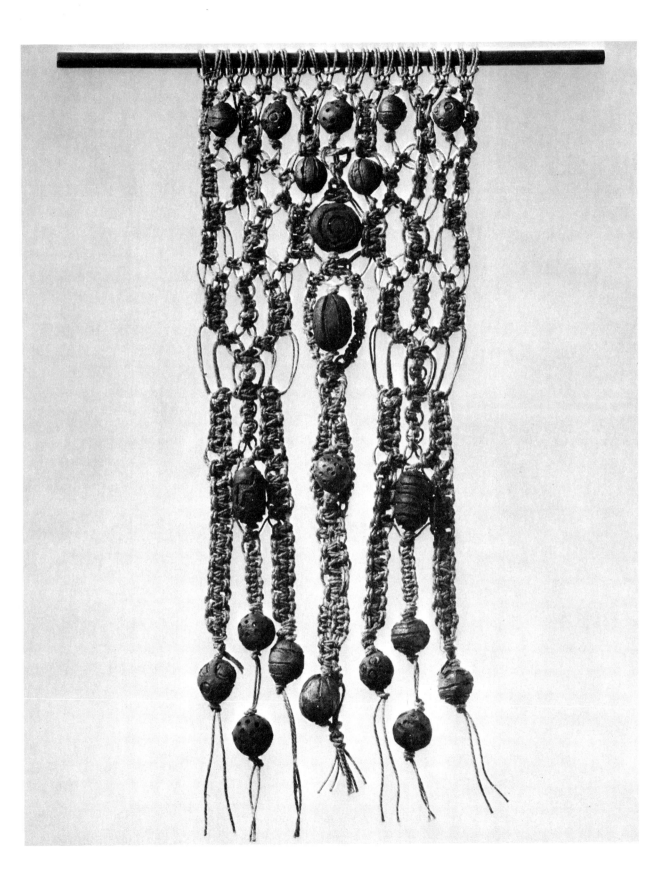

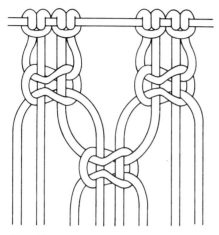

Knotting Pattern: Flat Knot
alternating

Detail of starting point, upper left corner,
showing variation of knots used

Placemat

The Flat Knot used in alternating rows is the featured knot in this project, as it was in the Shopping Bag (see pages 32–3), but here it is more closely tied, giving a totally different effect. The knot-bearing cord, worked into the edge Flat Knots so that no loose ends will be exposed, is an example of how to do an expert job, and also one of fine craftsmanship.

Size: 330 mm × 508 mm (13 in. × 20 in.).

Material: Orange thread.

Knots: Flat Knot and Cording.
Cut Ends: 52 ends, each 5·1 m (5 yd 20 in.) long.

Holding Cord: 3·6 m (4 yd).

Note: The holding cord is also the knot-bearing cord and is incorporated into the edge Flat Knot after being used for a row of Horizontal Cording, and all along the edge until needed again as a knot-bearing cord for the next row of Horizontal Cording. This will give three core ends, as shown in the diagram on the facing page.

To Begin: Tie an Overhand Knot about 26 mm (1 in.) in on the holding cord. Pin the knot securely to the board just before the beginning of a square and on a horizontal guideline. Using all the ends, do 1 row of Horizontal Cording (2 Heading, page 24). Return and do another row of Horizontal Cording.

Directions
1 row – Double Flat Knots
1 row – Horizontal Cording
3 rows – Flat Knots alternating
1 row – Horizontal Cording
1 row – Triple Flat Knots (sinnets)
1 row – Horizontal Cording
5 rows – Flat Knots alternating
1 row – Horizontal Cording
*7 rows – Flat Knots alternating
1 row – Horizontal Cording*
Repeat * to * seven times
1 row Horizontal Cording
5 rows – Flat Knots alternating
1 row – Horizontal Cording
3 rows – Flat Knots
1 row – Horizontal Cording
3 rows – Flat Knots alternating
1 row – Horizontal Cording
2 rows – Flat Knots
2 rows – Horizontal Cording

To Finish: With an embroidery needle or crochet hook, weave in the ends on the back side for at least 12 mm (½ in.). Trim. If the mat does not lay flat, pin it to size on the knotting board every 12 mm (½ in.). Spray lightly with water and allow it to dry.

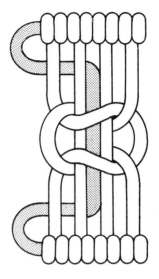

Flat Knot with three core ends. Third end is knot-bearer and is worked into edge Flat Knot until needed again

Orange placemat, 330 mm × 508 mm (13 in. × 20 in.)

Bracelets and Beads

Most of us have items around the house such as beads, buttons with shanks, and interesting belt buckles that have been stored safely away in boxes or jars. Such found objects can be combined effectively with Macramé. A few ideas are presented here.

bracelets

For holiday wear or gift-giving, here is a simple way to get new bracelets out of old ones.

Materials: Red, grey, dark green thread. Two bracelets, two bells

Knots: Flat Knot and Reversed Cording.

Cut Ends: Red and green – 1 end each, 3·1 m (3½ yd) long. Grey – 2 ends 3·1 m (3½ yd) long.

Directions for Red and Grey Bracelet: Hold edge of bracelet towards you and attach the red yarn with Reversed Cording so that the ends

Assortment of beads, buckles, bells, bracelets, and rings for use in Macramé pieces

come on the left side. Attach the grey in the same manner, except have the ends come on the right side.

The bracelet is now used as the core for the Flat Knot. Make tight Flat Knots around the bracelet until it is covered. Pull the ends through the beginning knots with a needle and hide them behind several knots before trimming ends.

Directions for Green and Grey Bracelet: Start as above, attaching green and grey ends to bracelet. With Reversed Cording alternate colours until bracelet is covered. Attach bells to the green and grey ends before tucking the ends in and trimming off.

neckpiece

This idea for a neckpiece is an attractive way to use beads from that broken necklace. You could also make a beaded sash or bracelet. Buttons with shanks can be used in the same manner.

Materials are thread and beads of two sizes. The small beads were put onto a holding cord and alternated with Reversed Cording. The piece consists of beads of two sizes, Flat and Overhand Knots and a combination of the two, and Half Knots.

Adding on Beads: If you are adding wooden beads and the holes are too small for the ends to go through, use a needle to enlarge them. Apply fixative to ends to help pass them through the holes.

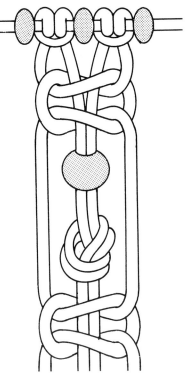

One way of arranging beads

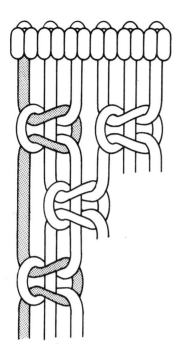

Knotting pattern

Hand bobbins shown on the piece being worked

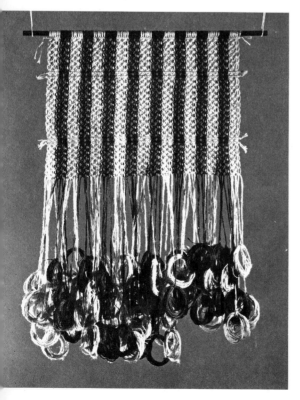

Room Divider

Two versions of the Flat Knot are used here, one with a multiple of three double ends, the other using four double ends. Either version, using separately or in combination, creates a unique and interesting pattern. The dimensions for the room divider are given as 508 mm × 1,524 mm (20 in. × 60 in.) but of course alter them to whatever size you need. You may also wish to use a different yarn; jute would be very effective.

Size: 508 mm × 1,524 mm (20 in. × 60 in.).

Materials: Natural and black thread. The yarn is double. 660 mm (26 in.) black dowel

Knots: Flat Knot and Horizontal Cording

Cut Ends: Natural – 54 ends, each 8·2 m (9 yd) long.
Black – 48 ends, each 8·2 m (9 yd) long.

Knot-bearing Cord: For each row of Horizontal Cording, cut two ends, each 660 mm (26 in.) long.

Note: The Flat Knots are made with three ends doubled as shown in the diagram. Always start these knots on the left side. Reverse direction of each row of Horizontal Cording; that is, if 1st row began on left side, start next row on right side.

To Begin: Tie a row of Reversed Cording onto the dowel. Make a row of Horizontal Cording on the knot-bearing cord, using doubled ends.

Directions:
*1 Do 1 row Flat Knots
2 Drop first end on left, and do 1 row Flat Knots.* There will be two free ends at end of row.
Repeat * to * 5 times, ending with row 1.
Do 1 row Horizontal Cording, 1 row Flat Knots, 1 row Horizontal Cording.
Repeat * to * 10 times, ending with row 1.
Repeat ** to **.
Repeat * to * 10 times, ending with row 1.
For a more open effect, one with more scale, make the Flat Knot with four ends used as one.

To Finish: Individual taste is best here. Suggestions include trimming ends off neatly for a fringe effect, or making individual sinnets.

A dowel can also be used at the bottom, as it was at the top, particularly if you want the piece to remain taut in the width.

Cushion Cover

There are two interesting features to this project. One is the pattern created by the Flat Knot in alternating rows; the other is the use of two yarns that are closely related in colour but contrast greatly in texture. Two patterns are given for back and front of the same cushion cover or for separate cushion covers.

Size: 254 mm × 254 mm (10 in. × 10 in.).

Materials: Red rug wool. Red thread.

Knots: Flat Knot and Horizontal Cording.

Cut Ends: Rug Wool – 24 ends, each 3·1 m (3 yd 9 in.) long.
Coarse thread: 12 ends, each 3·5 m (3yd 28 in.) long.

Holding Cord: Used also as knot-bearing cord
Cut 5·5 m (6 yd) of rug wool.

Note: All Flat Knots are double in this piece.
Arrange the ends as follows before beginning to knot:
16 wool, 12 thread, 16 wool, 12 thread, 16 wool.

Directions

For one side of cushion cover:
*Do 2 rows Horizontal Cording (3 heading, page 24). Make small picots.

Turn work over. Do 2 rows Horizontal Cording. Turn work over again. Do 1 row Horizontal Cording.*
**1 row, Double Flat Knots
1 row, Flat Knots alternating. At each edge of this row do Reversed Cording.
1 row, Double Flat Knots.
1 row, Horizontal Cording.
Turn work over. Do 1 row Horizontal Cording.
Turn work over again. Do 1 row Horizontal Cording.**
Repeat ** to ** 4 times.
Repeat first 3 rows of Flat Knots.
Repeat * to *. This completes the first side.

Continue knotting for second side:

Do 27 rows Double Flat Knots alternating, as shown in diagram.

To Finish: On reverse side, pull each two ends through the beginning loops, then thread the ends through the Horizontal Cording.
Cut off excess ends. Sew one side. Reverse and insert cushion. Sew fourth side.

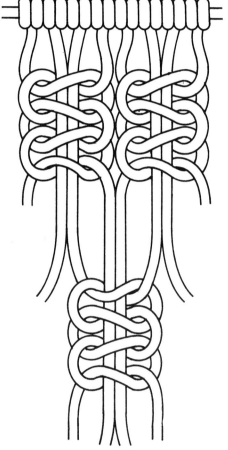

Knotting pattern: Double Flat Knot alternating

(*Left*) Front of red cushion cover worked in two different yarns. Note horizontal rows separating Flat Knot areas

(*Right*) Back of red cushion cover (also shown in detail on page 28). Note diagonal pattern created by Flat Knots worked in alternate rows

Two Examples from Mitla

The way in which knots are used determines the density of closely drawn knotted areas or the openness of unknotted areas. Two good examples of open-work are shown here in the colourful sash to the left and the stole on the facing page. They were knotted by Indians of Mitla, a town in the State of Oaxaca, Mexico. Both were made with handspun wools, as is much of the Macramé work from Mitla. The wool is mostly from sheep in the area and, although occasionally dyed, is usually left in its natural colour.

Sash. The hand-dyed colours in the sash are bold and gay. Rows of crossed Diagonal Cording are worked only at intervals and form a kind of network to hold the loose scallop-shaped ends together, giving the piece an orderly well-defined pattern.

Triangular and diamond-shaped designs make a strong appearance, and the spots of colour at the crossings of the threads accentuate an exceptionally attractive design.

Stole. The stole is very luxurious-looking and has a lacy charm. Its loose airiness almost makes one unaware of the fact that every detail in it has been carefully developed. Very often these handsome stoles, which the Indians call *rebozos*, are done in a combination of colours similar to those used in the sash. Also, from this area of Mexico, stoles are worked, like the sash, completely in the Cording technique.

This particular stole, however, is in natural wool and uses the Mitla version of the Half Knot to make the half-diamond bands and the diamond areas within which other diamonds are contained. In the centre of the small diamonds, Overhand Knots are worked, thus demonstrating still another technique of creating an open area.

The fringe is made row by row, using an Overhand Knot in an alternate arrangement to tie each group of ends.

(*Left*) Detail of multicolour sash made by Indians of Mitla, Mexico. The wool is handspun, and is worked in crossed Diagonal Cording

(*Facing page*) Detail of stole in natural hand-spun wool—another example of open Macramé work from Mitla

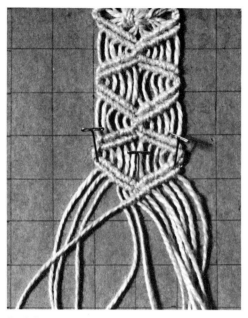

Sash is shown pinned to knotting board and against guidelines to keep proper width. Note method of crossing for Diagonal Cording

Sash 1 (Jute Sash)

To make a sash inspired by the work of the Mitla Indians, the Diagonal Cording and the Flat Knot with multi-ends are used. This combination is a useful and attractive way to achieve an open effect and an interesting pattern. The result is a handsome sash with weight and substance, and with somewhat the character of homespun work.

Size: 50 mm × 2,032 mm (2 in. × 80 in.) including fringes.

Materials: 1 cone Jute-Tone. 1 Chalk white.
Knots: Horizontal and Diagonal Cording, Flat Knot using 10 ends, Double Chain Knot.

Cut Ends: 7 ends, each 8·5 m (9 yd) long. No holding cord.

Directions: For the beginning fringe, make up 203 m (8 in.) Double Chain Knot sinnets with every two ends – see example 9, pages 18–19. With the middle two ends, take one end to the right. Make Horizontal Double Cording across the row and back again to the middle. Repeat on left side.

Pattern: *Make a diamond with 2 rows of Diagonal Cording.*

**Make the top half of diamond. With centre 10 ends make a Flat Knot, using 2,6,2. Complete diamond ** (A reminder: 2,6,2 means using 2 ends on either side and 6 ends as the core ends.)

Repeat * to *	Repeat ** to ** 3 times
Repeat ** to ** 3 times	Repeat * to * 3 times
Repeat * to * 3 times	Repeat ** to ** 3 times
Repeat ** to ** 5 times	Repeat * to * 3 times
Repeat * to * 3 times	Repeat ** to ** 5 times
Repeat ** to ** 3 times	Repeat * to *
Repeat * to * 3 times	

To Finish: Repeat the 2 rows of Horizontal Cording, made as in the beginning, and the 203 mm (8 in.) Double Chain Knot sinnets with every two ends.

(*Below*) Mitla-inspired sash made in jute—detail shown in actual size. Note that in some diamond areas the centres are gathered into a multiend Flat Knot

Sash 2 (Multicolour Sash)

This vivid three-coloured sash, in a repeat diagonal design, is achieved primarily with the Diagonal Cording Knot worked in a closely knotted pattern on both sides. An additional feature of this sash is the decorative use of the bobble.

This sash may be made as long as you wish by repeating the pattern.

Materials: Orange thread. Rug wool. Rose and black.

Knots: Diagonal Cording, Flat Knot, Overhand Knot, and Bobble.

Width: Rose and orange – 4 ends each. Black – 2 ends.

Arrange ends as follows, pinning each loop:
    2 black, 4 rose, 8 orange, 4 rose, 2 black
    Leave 356 m (14 in.) free before beginning to knot.

Multicolour sash with bobbles. The piece is worked on both sides with the Diagonal Cording. The diagonal ridges are caused by working on the right side, the dotted pattern by working on the reverse side

Directions: For beginning section.

With outside black end do Diagonal Cording to centre. Repeat with black end on other side.

Cross the two ends where they meet and continue in this manner for 3 rows, which brings four ends in rose to middle.

Make a bobble with the four centre ends in rose, using 5 Flat Knots (see diagram).

Continue with the Diagonal Cording for 8 more rows. (This brings the four black ends to the middle.)

Make a bobble, using 5 Flat Knots.

Turn piece over. Continue with Diagonal Cording for 8 rows.

Turn piece over. Make an orange bobble.

Pattern Repeat: * Turn piece over. Do 10 rows Diagonal Cording.* Continue * to * until centre section is of desired length. **Note**: Be sure to turn piece every 10 rows.

Directions: For ending section.

Make an orange bobble. Turn piece over and do 6 rows Diagonal Cording.

Turn piece over and make a rose bobble.

Turn piece over and do 4 rows Diagonal Cording.

Turn piece to front and do 2 rows Diagonal Cording.

Make a black bobble. Continue with Diagonal Cording until there are 10 rows in all.

To Finish: Make Flat Knot sinnets with remaining ends and tie them with a Gathering Knot.

MAKING A BOBBLE

Bobbles can be made to any size by changing the length of the Flat Knot sinnet. They can also be made with multi-end Flat Knots. See diagram for construction.

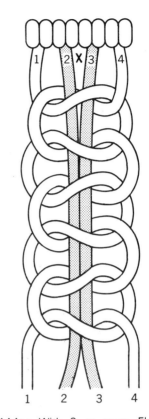

Bobble: With 3 or more Flat Knots, make a sinnet. Bring core ends up to the beginning of the sinnet between ends 2 and 3 and draw through the space marked X. A crochet hook may be necessary. Pull core ends down firmly to complete bobble. Continue with whatever knot the pattern calls for

Beginning of Belt 1. (*Below*) With four ends make No. 5 heading (page 24). Lay a new end over the Flat Knot. Tie it in with a row of Horizontal Cordings, using all the ends. Take another end and continue in this fashion until there are twelve ends

Belt 1

Two belts are presented here. In the first you will be using another technique – the adding on of extra ends in order to widen a piece.

Finished Length: 864 mm (34 in.). (For a longer or shorter belt, extend or reduce pattern areas.)

Materials: Natural thread. 2 loop buckles.

Cut Ends: 6 ends, each 7·3 m (8 yd) long.

Knots: Flat Knot and Horizontal Cording.

To Begin: For construction of the beginning, see diagram at left.

Directions: * Do 6 rows Flat Knots alternating.
Do 6 rows Double Flat Knots alternating.
Make three sinnets of 6 Flat Knots each.
Do 6 Reversed Flat Knots on the two end threads on each side.
Make two sinnets of 6 Flat Knots each, using the 8 remaining ends.
Make three sinnets of 6 Flat Knots each.*
Repeat * to *
Do 6 rows Flat Knots alternating.
Do 6 rows Double Flat Knots alternating.
Make three sinnets of 6 Flat Knots each.

To Finish: Cut remaining ends, leaving about 152 mm (6 in.). Put the ends over the loop buckles, with the back side of the belt facing you. Pull each four ends through each Flat Knot. Tie each two ends with an Overhand Knot. Cut off remaining ends. When you put the beginning of the belt through the loop, the right side will show.

The last part of Belt 2

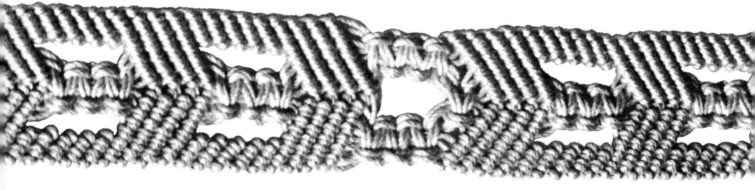

The last part of Belt 1

Belt 2

You make this belt to any length by following the directions.

Materials: Natural thread.

Knots and Key: Horizontal, Diagonal and Reversed Cording – HC, DC, RC. Flat Knot using multi-ends – FK. Diagonal Cording crossing in middle – DCX.

Width: Cut 8 ends.

To Begin: Follow diagram.

Directions: 3 rows DCX, 5 rows DC
* 3 FK in the middle, tied 2,4,2. On either side do 5 rows DC knotted with four ends *
2 rows DCX
Repeat * to *
** 4 rows DCX **
Repeat * to *, repeat ** to **
§ Make two sinnets of 3 FK each tied 2,4,2. Add 1 FK made with centre ends, 2,4,2 §
Repeat ** to **, * to * as many times as necessary to complete back section for length desired, ending with ** to **.
Repeat: § to §–** to **–* to *–** to **–* to *–** to **–* to * 1 row DCX, 3 rows DC, 4 rows DCX. 1 row HC as follows: cross ends in middle; take one end horizontally to the right and one end horizontally to the left.

To Finish: Put all ends over right buckle. Pull each end through to the back into the row of HC. Tie every four ends in a very tight Overhand Knot. Put Uhu glue over knot. When it dries, cut ends.

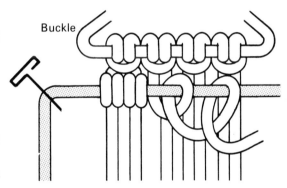

The beginning of Belt 2. Put seven ends onto left buckle, using Reversed Cording. With remaining end, do row of Horizontal Cording as shown in the diagram. (*Below*) Starting point can be seen on finished belt on right side of buckle

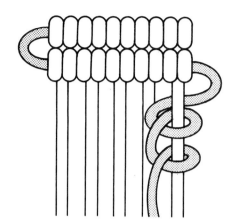

Vertical Cording are used to change colour from gold to blue

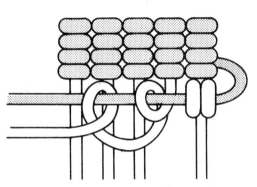

Method for changing colour from blue to gold

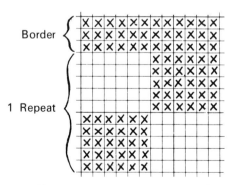

Key: X's = Horizontal Cording. White squares = Vertical Cording

Rugs

Cording, when worked in a closely knotted pattern using coarse thread and/or wool as the yarns, produces sturdy and long-wearing mats and rugs. Because the knotting is kept simple, colours can play a large role in the design. Note, in the blue and gold rug section at right, how the Horizontal and Vertical Cording create a chequerboard pattern and how vivid the ridged effects of these knots are. Both the front and back of the work are shown; either could be considered as the right side. The diagrams at left show how to change colours to achieve the pattern.

The use of this knot also makes it possible to chart a design on graph paper. Before making a graph, make samples so that you will know the amount of ends to 25 mm (1 in.).

The directions below are for a rug section of the size 241 mm × 381 mm (9½ in. × 15 in.). By adding to the length and width of the ends and by repeating the pattern, you can make any size desired. It is also possible to make a rug by working just in sections, and then joining them. Sections can be also made in squares.

blue and gold rug

Size: 241 mm × 381 mm (9½ in. × 15 in.) section

Materials: Rug wool. Blue 750, gold 17.

Cut Ends: Gold – 42, each 3·0 m (3 yd 12 in.) long.

Holding Cord: Blue – 185·6 m (203 yd) long, used also as knot-bearing cord. It will be necessary to splice this cord, since this amount of yarn will be too unwieldy for one butterfly. Cut the cord into sections and wind into butterflies.

Knots and Key: Horizontal and Vertical Cording – HC, VC.

To Begin: Attach 3 rows HC to holding cord, using heading 2 (page 24).

Directions: * 6 HC, 6 VC. Repeat 3 times across row. End with 6 HC*
Repeat * to * 5 times.
** 6 VC, 6 HC. Repeat 3 times across row, ending with 6 VC **
Repeat ** to ** 5 times.
Repeat * to * and ** to ** 5 times.
Repeat * to.*
3 rows HC.

To Finish: Turn piece over. Thread in ends as shown in photograph.

Front

Back

Method for threading in ends
with embroidery needle

red rug

The red rug section in three colours shown here has the same chequer-board pattern as in the blue and gold rug section, but it is somewhat more advanced in technique. It also differs in the method of working, which affords a different surface texture. Again the variations and effects possible with the Cording Knot are evident. The Horizontal and Vertical versions are used, and the variation is achieved by knotting from the front and then from the back. The end result makes the additional effort well worth while. The tying cords are of two colours, red and fuchsia; the third colour, plum, is used as the knot-bearing cord. This rug section can be made by following the graph shown.

Size: 127 mm × 350 mm (5 in. × 14 in.) section, including fringe.

Material: Rug wool. Fuchsia 239, red 242, plum 610.

Cut Ends: Fuchsia–6 ends, each 2·8 m (3 yd 4 in.) long.
Red–6 ends, each 2·8 m (3 yd 4 in.) long.
Plum–5·5 m (6 yd), for knot-bearing cord.
Each colour area is knotted in the manner keyed by the graph.

KEY

HC = Horizontal Cording
VC = Vertical Cording

———	HC knotted on front–1st colour
– – – –	HC knotted on front–2nd colour
●	HC knotted on back–1st colour
·	HC knotted on back–2nd colour
<	VC knotted on front–3rd colour
o	HC knotted on back–3rd colour

(*Facing page*) Red rug section. Each colour area is knotted as indicated in the graph at upper right. Note that the pattern is worked on both front and back sides of the piece for added textural interest

Helpful Hint–To solve the problem of handling yarn in large bulk when making a larger rug section of heavy wool, you can knot from the centre and work from two directions. First work in one direction. This means that the wound ends do not have to be as long and awkward to handle as they would be if the rug were worked from one side only. The photograph at right shows the method for beginning the section

Cavandoli Stitch

The patterns on these two pages are examples of Macramé worked in the Cavandoli Stitch; information about the origin and background of this work is to be found in the Introduction. It consists of closely worked knotting in two colours. Just the Horizontal and Vertical Cordings are used–the former for background, the latter for design. This work is unique and will enable you to chart and knot geometric shapes, trees, flowers, figures and so on to wherever your skill and imagination take you. Note the bird and plant figures on the Cavandoli-worked border for the Italian bag (see also page 6). A different-styled bird, influenced by a Mexican silver pin decoration, is presented in the graph below right. The graph at left shows the possibility of obtaining a circular pattern effect. The curves are within the squares and are illusionary.

Border pattern for Italian bag in Cavandoli Stitch (bag is illustrated on page 6)

Bird Pattern

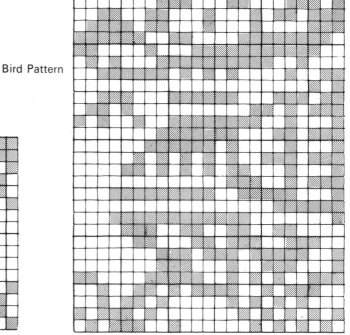

Circular Pattern

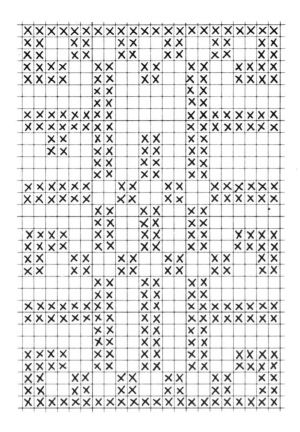

Geometric pattern. X's = Horizontal Cording; white squares = Vertical Cording

black and white rug

The graph above is for the rug pattern and can be worked in different sizes. It is the simplest of the three graphs and is given with additional information. On all graphs, the dark areas represent the Horizontal Cordings and the light areas the Vertical Cordings. Note how identically the finished rug section pattern matches the graph.

Size: 102 mm × 152 mm (4 in. × 6 in.) section

Materials: Black thread.
    Avanti rug wool. White.

Cut Ends: Black—11 ends, each 1,119 mm (48 in.) long.

Holding Cord, used also as knot-bearing cord: White, 3·6 m (4 yd) long.

To Begin: Attach ends to holding cord with 2 heading (page 24). In the 1st row the black cords are tied over the white cord. From then on go according to the graph so that sometimes you are tying black over white, and at other times white over black, depending on how the pattern is charted.

To Finish: Repeat the first row and make any fringe to your liking. The reverse side is equally handsome and, depending upon the effect you want, can be used for the right side.

Wall-Hanging or Handbag

The project presented here can be used in one of two ways: either as a wall hanging, or, with the sides attached, as a handsome handbag. As in Sash 2 (page 48), the strong colours are used as contrasting bands that meet in the centre and cross. The solid areas of the pattern are worked in the Diagonal Cording (page 21, diagram D), and textural relief is supplied by the Flat Knot.

Size: 191 mm × 308 mm (7½ in. × 20 in.)

Materials: Rug wool. Red, white, and black.
2 black dowels, 241 mm (9¼ in.) long.

Cut Ends: Red—10 ends, each 5·5 m (6 yd) long.
Black—10 ends, each 5·5 m (6 yd) long.
White—8 ends, each 5·5 m (6 yd) long.

Knots: Flat Knot and Diagonal Cording.

To Begin: Arrange colours for knotting in this order: Red, white, black. Leave about 102 mm (4 in.) of yarn before making sinnets of 6 Flat Knots, using four ends each.

Directions to make top section:
Do 1 row Flat Knots.
Drop two ends on each side and do 1 row Flat Knots.
Continue making rows of Flat Knots, dropping two ends on each row until the last Flat Knot is made from the middle four ends. This will make a triangular area.

To continue:
Pick up the dropped ends and make 20 rows of Diagonal Cording with the ends crossing in the middle. (See pages 22–3 for angling technique.)

Turn piece over. Do 8 rows Diagonal Cording crossing in the middle.

Turn piece over. Do 28 rows Diagonal Cording. The knotted area now comes to a point. With the remaining ends on each side, fill in the areas with Flat Knots until the piece is even across.

Make Flat Knot sinnets as in the beginning.
Put sinnets over rods at both ends and thread ends in.

To Finish: Line with black cotton fabric, or colour of your choice. For purse, sew sides 140 mm (5½ in.) on each side.

Detail of finished bag

Handles

Material: Black wool.

Cut Ends: 4 ends, each 1,119 mm (48 in.) long.

Directions: With two ends make loops and attach with Reversed Cording between 2nd and 3rd loops on dowel. The core ends should be 356 mm (14 in.) long; the outside ends, 864 mm (34 in.) long.

Make a sinnet of Flat Knots, 305 (12 in.) long. Loop sinnet over the rod, between last two loops; draw ends through to secure.

Repeat for second handle.

Same wall-hanging becomes a handbag when sides are sewn together and handles are affixed

(*Left*) Macramé piece used as wall-hanging, with dowels at top and bottom

Wall-Hangings

It is hoped that these Macramé pieces will help in creating designs. To help further, 'Christmas Bells', pages 70–71, is given with full directions. All others are analysed so that you may see how knots are combined and progress in their many variations. Note that the hangings are bi-symmetrical: whatever is worked on one side is also worked on the other.

spirit of '76

159 mm × 686 mm (6¼ in. × 27 in.).

The wall-hanging in red, white, and blue rug wool on the facing page could be considered an exercise in angling and colour (see pages 22–3). The knots used were the Flat Knot and the Horizontal Cording. The piece was started on a wooden bar and its knotting was duplicated for the ending. The colours are all strong in value so that they provide good contrast where they cross. The pattern was kept simple to avoid any conflict with the colours.

All the colours are easy to follow, but, taking the white as an example, note how it starts in the middle, separates towards the right and left, and disappears only to reappear and repeat the pattern.

By the continuation of Horizontal Cording rows, the white was worked at the end to the right and left. Sinnets were made of each colour, and a holding cord was added, onto which three rows of Horizontal Cording were made. The ends were trimmed, giving a plain fringe consistent with the simplicity of the piece.

amigo

140 mm × 838 mm (5½ in. × 33 in.)

The colour of handmade wooden beads from Morelia, Mexico, contributed handsomely towards the design of Amigo (*right*) and harmonized with the brown and natural thread. The beads were used in the heading along with Double Flat Knots. Brown thread was introduced during rows of Horizontal and Vertical Cording. The beads in the middle were added between Triple Flat Knots. Construction continued, using the above knots and more beads.

The ending could be a simple piece by itself. Two rows of Horizontal Cording precede a triangle of Flat Knots. These are enclosed by Diagonal Cording. The sinnets at the finish are ended with Flat Knots and are pulled together with a Gathering Knot.

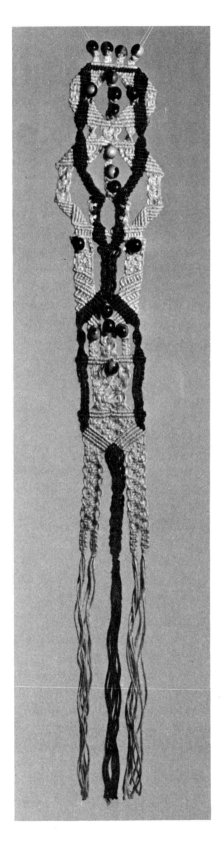

bill's folly

152 mm × 254 mm (6 in. × 10 in.)
Collection of the Penland School of Crafts

This hanging (*left*), in three colours, is a good exercise for beginners. Flat Knots with multi-ends and Horizontal Cording were used. It could be very welcome as a thank-you present or as a baby christening gift.

The yarns are natural thread and rug wool. A flat bar of hardwood was used in place of a holding cord to mount the starting ends. The sides were knotted in Horizontal Cording. The centre repeated the Horizontal Cording pattern, and a bobble (see page 49) was knotted in for additional interest. To the right and left of the centre, multi-end Flat Knots were made, followed by rows of Flat Knots and an area of Horizontal Cording angled.

For the finish the piece was pulled together by two rows of Horizontal Cording. Sinnets were made with Flat Knots, ending with an Overhand Knot.

animal fair

Approx. 50 mm × 457 mm (2 in. × 18 in.)

The three wall-hangings on the facing page were made with children in mind and were presented to my nephew and two nieces for Christmas. The oldest child was then six years old.

The materials used were plied linen and lightweight rug wool. Each piece is different, but they all have the following knots in common: Flat Knots, Overhand Knots, Reversed, Vertical, Diagonal and Horizontal Cording, and bobbles.

The pieces were started on wooden napkin rings hand-carved into animal shapes by craftsmen in North Carolina. Searching out and using items of handicraft, such as these, brings excitement and pleasure to the knotter as well as contributing a new dimension to the work.

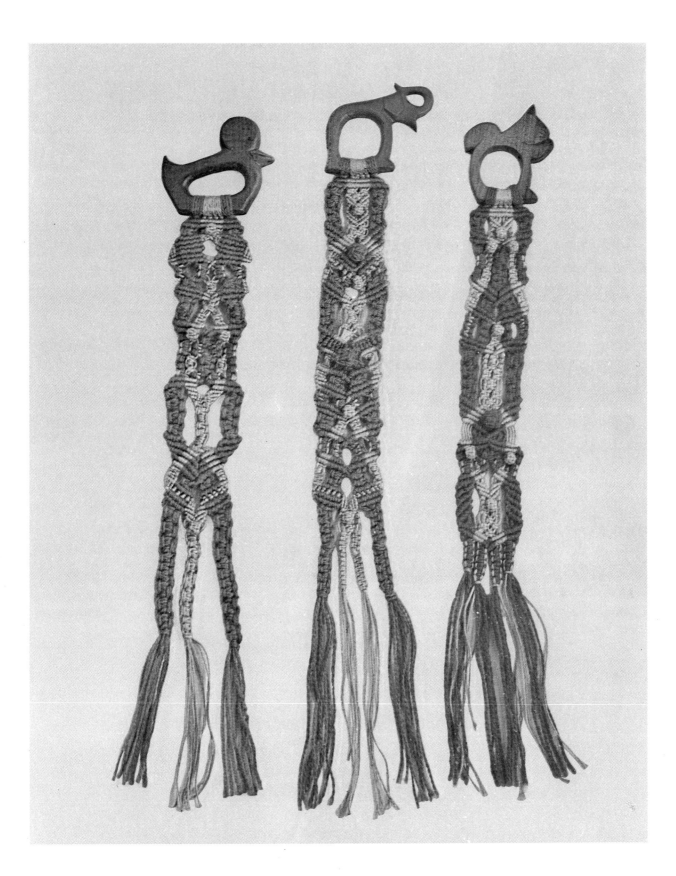

peking

203 mm × 1,397 mm (8 in. × 55 in.)
Collection of Mrs Glenn A. Stackhouse

Another approach to consider is combining interesting old jewellery with yarns as illustrated by the wall-hanging on these pages. Old Peking glass beads of two sizes, a bracelet, and a ring were used. This piece is among my favourites because it was an adventure just to find the beads hidden under a counter and in the basement of one of the old shops in San Francisco's Chinatown. The bracelet and ring were found in still another fascinating shop. With these adornments as starting points, I used a matching colour in thread to further enhance the beads for the design I had planned.

The piece was started on the small ring using Reversed Cording. Two rows of Horizontal Cordings followed, then a row of Flat Knots. Five small beads were added. Additional knotting was done before the bracelet was added. All the ends were then attached by a row of Horizontal Cording, and the top part of the wall-hanging was completed.

The work progressed by keeping the sides and centre as separate points of interest. On the right and left sides, beads were put on, then flanked by Reversed Cording going into rows of Horizontal Cording; these were followed by Flat Knots and Overhand Knots, all ending in a section of Horizontal Cording. The centre section used beads in two different sizes and narrow bands of Horizontal Cording.

The piece was then brought together by a couple of rows of Horizontal Cording and a small bead, followed by narrow bands worked in variations on the Horizontal Cording. Flat Knots and Overhand Knots were then worked, divided by rows of Horizontal Cording.

Three sections again became separate units. In the centre, narrow bands of Horizontal Cording were made, and beads, divided by Flat Knots, were added. On the outside areas, alternating and crossing bands of Cording were angled. This section was ended with Flat Knots, Overhand Knots, then small units of Horizontal Cording, followed by several rows done in the same knot.

Again the piece divided into three sections. Cording, angling and crossing, are on the outside, and in the centre are Flat Knots, Overhand Knots, Horizontal and Reversed Cording, and beads of two sizes.

(*Left*) Detail of heading section of Peking, showing how ends were mounted onto a small ring. Note the colour blend of both the yarn and the jewellery pieces

(*Below*) Detail of centre section. Note alternating and crossing bands of angled Cording on outside areas. Horizontal Cording join this section at beginning and end

The section that follows could be considered for a separate wall-hanging. Rows of Horizontal Cording, Flat Knots, Overhand Knots, and twisted Half Knots form borders for rows of small beads.

The last section is in three parts. The outside areas begin by crossing and progress to Flat Knots and Overhand Knots in alternating sections. The centre has a diamond area of Double Flat Knots. These go into solid areas of Horizontal Cording with a bead in the middle. The entire section is held together with several rows of Horizontal Cording.

Travelling downwards, the side and centre sections were formed into open areas by Double Flat Knots, and Flat Knots with Overhand Knots. Rows of Horizontal Cording also were worked. The side sections progressed to crossed areas divided by Double Flat Knots and Horizontal Cording. The centre progressed from Flat Knots and Overhand Knots to Horizontal Cording interspersed with beads. The ends are sinnets of Flat Knots and twisting Half Knots and embrace the same principle as the ending of Amigo on page 61.

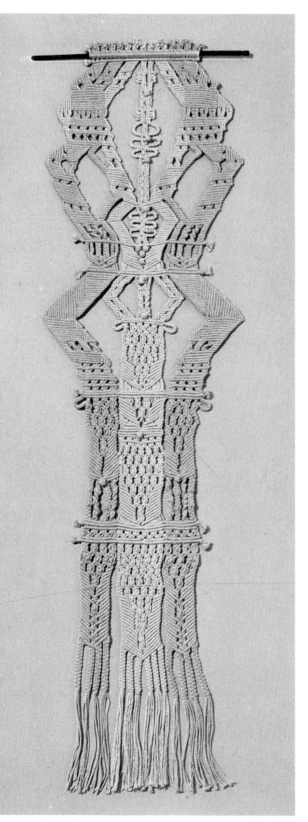

empress

241 mm × 838 mm (9½ in. × 33 in.)

Picots, prominently placed in the top half of the centre area, contribute a looped ribbon effect to this wall-hanging.

Still another specific decorative approach is added by bobbles and more picots appearing occasionally on the edges. The yarns used are yellow linen and natural silk cord. The piece was started with No 5 (see page 24), a crownlike effect which served to introduce and to accentuate the picot theme. After being knotted, the heading was mounted onto an old teak chopstick.

The centre section, in the natural silk twist, besides being worked in a variety of picots and bobbles, also contains Flat Knots, Overhand Knots, and Reversed Cording. In addition, there are angled areas of Cording. The side areas in yellow linen are dominated by angling Cording, Flat Knots, Half Knots, Overhand Knots, and sinnets of Half Knots that twist in opposite directions.

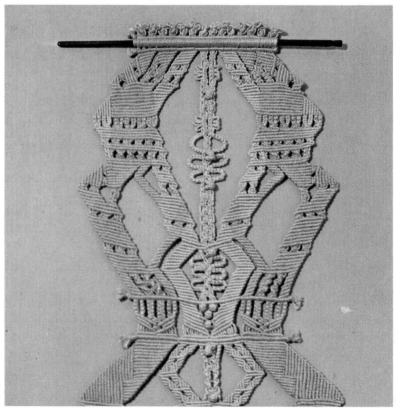

(*Above*) Enlarged detail of top section, showing the decorative use of picots and bobbles

In the bottom half of the hanging, the yellow and white areas appear separate, but while the colours are independent of each other, the design is not. The beginning of this area is a good example of the variations that can be obtained by angling the Cording. As stated previously, the Half Hitch is the most practical knot for obtaining variations.

The knots used here are the same as those worked in the top half of the piece, but the effect is a constrasting one due to the arrangement of the design. The top was worked as if the sections were independent of one another, although the knots formed a continuous and similar pattern, whereas the knots in the bottom half were worked straight across the rows to form a unit. The piece ends in Flat Knot sinnets.

summer sun

152 mm × 888 mm (6 in × 35 in.)
Collection of the Penland School of Crafts

One of the unique features of this wall-hanging is the development of its shape from a narrow heading at the top to an increased width as the piece is worked. The addition of extra ends throughout the growth of the top half accounts for its gradual widening. This technique, which was used in Belt 1 (page 50–51), is a practical one in Macramé work for developing small rounded or pointed areas.

The yarns used are rug wool and linen thread, both in different shades of yellow. The piece was started on a Peking glass ring which immediately limited the number of starting ends that could be used effectively. In the top half, the edges were developed in wool, and the remaining area in linen. In the linen area, additional ends were put on to begin increasing the width of the piece. Additional ends were also put on in the wool areas and were used in Vertical Cording next to rows of Horizontal Cording. Bobbles were interspersed for added textural interest.

Separate sinnets were made of linen and of wool and of a combination of the two materials. The crossed area was done in a combination of Horizontal Cording and sinnets, and multi-end Flat Knots. The rest of the piece was made up of variations on the Horizontal Cording and Flat Knot. The piece was finished with sinnets, each made up of a variation on the knots used.

stately mansion

191 mm × 966 mm (7½ in. × 42 in.)

Two distinguishable design elements are very evident here, and they are further accentuated by the rows of Horizontal Cording that serve to separate them. The angling technique of Cording (see pages 22–3) makes the planning of distinctive pieces possible and by its use clearly illustrates how Macramé work can be developed to express an idea, much like a painting. This wall-hanging is presented as an excellent example of the use of this knot in one of its many variations.

The yarns were two kinds of silk used double, wool singly, and linen thread. The knots were the Cording in its many variations, and the Flat Knot for making bobbles.

The first patterned design appears in the top section of the piece and consists firstly of three areas of Flat Knot bobbles in wool. These are interspersed with other areas made up of crisscrossed bands done by varying the Horizontal Cording. The combination of these two different knotted areas results in a strong diamond effect which looks as though it had been interwoven. This section can be seen in detail in the upper photograph on the facing page. Following the area described, more crisscrossed bands were worked and were held together with rows of Horizontal Cording.

The second design area was worked in a manner completely different from any of the other hangings that have been shown. Note that the lower detail photograph on the facing page clearly shows the twisted areas of this unique pattern. By working variations on the Horizontal Cording throughout this entire piece, it was possible to knot what appears as three different columns, all made with separate twists. For the centre column, two strips were knotted separately, then twisted, and then knotted again with the Horizontal Cording travelling in different directions, until they were knotted together to form one column.

The two columns on the sides were each composed of two different-sized strips. Each pair of strips was knotted separately until they reached a midpoint where they were joined. They continued to grow with Diagonal Cording until they, and the centre column, met at the beginning of the next section.

More areas of crisscrossed bands were accomplished by working the Horizontal Cording in a partial repeat of the first design. This was followed by a repeat with variations on the second design. Either of these two designs could be chosen to make an effective smaller hanging, or they could be a starting point for your own ideas.

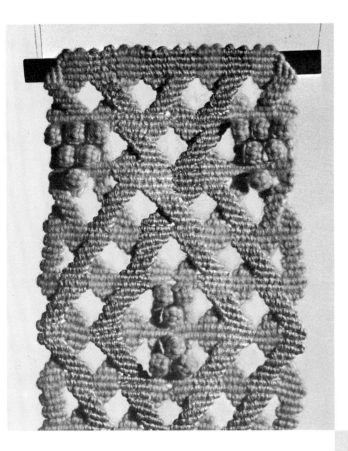

(*Left*) Detail of top section of Stately Mansion clearly shows the angling technique of the Cording (explained on pages 22–3). Bobbles are clustered for added decorative effect

(*Right*) Detail of centre section, showing how six bands were joined together at midpoint to make three columns. Note twist of centre column

christmas bells

This gay holiday wall hanging is presented with full directions. The important feature here is in the play of colour between the red and green bands, and the contrast between the solid areas of knotting and the open spaces. Both the knotting pattern and the design were kept simple so as not to conflict with the colours.

Size: 114 mm × 1,145 mm (4¼ in × 49 in.)

Materials: Red, grey, moss green thread. 19 brass bells

Cut Ends: 4 ends of each colour, each 20·1 m (22 yds) long.

Holding Cord, also used as knot-bearing cord: 1 end of grey, 457 mm (18 in.) long.

Knots and Key: Flat Knot–FK, and Horizontal, Diagonal, Vertical and Reversed Cording–HC, DC, VC, RC. Diagonal Cording Crossing–DCX.

Top section. Note triangular area of Flat Knots and how dropped ends were worked into diagonal rows of Cording

Detail shows colour changes from one side to the other and open areas

To Begin: Make Flat Knots on a holding cord (No. 4 heading, page 24), using 8 red, 8 grey and 8 green.

Do 2 rows HC.

Do 1 row across of HC in red, VC in grey, and HC in green.

Do 1 row HC.

The beginning of the piece is now completed.

Directions: Do 1 row FK, drop two ends on each side, and do another row FK. Continue in this manner, dropping two ends on each side until 1 FK is left.

Put a bell on the core ends of the last knot.

This completes the triangle of Flat Knots.

Pick up the dropped ends and do 4 rows DCX.

Do 1 row FK.

Do 4 rows DCX.

* In the centre, put two bells onto core ends of green and red. Do 1 row FK, 2 rows DCX; put bell on the two ends that cross. Do 2 rows DCX. Do 1 row FK.*

8 rows DCX, repeat * to *	4 rows DC
8 rows DC	1 row FK
1 row FK	4 rows DC, repeat * to *
4 rows DC, repeat * to *	6 rows DCX
8 rows DCX	1 row FK
1 row FK	4 rows DCX
4 rows DC	1 row FK
1 row FK	4 rows DCX
8 rows DC, repeat * to *	1 row FK
8 rows DCX	8 rows DCX, repeat * to *
1 row FK	4 rows DCX
4 rows DC	1 row FK
1 row FK	8 rows DCX

Fringe to finish off piece, using variation on Flat Knots

To Finish: Make the fringe by first travelling from the left to the middle in the following manner:

3 FK–red	2 FK–(2 red and 2 grey ends)
1 FK–grey	2 FK–(2 grey and 2 green ends)
1 FK–green	4 FK–each of red, grey, and green
2 FK–(2 red and 2 grey ends)	2 RC–red
2 RC–red	2 FK–(2 red and 2 grey ends)
2 FK–(2 red and 2 grey ends)	2 FK–(2 grey and 2 green ends)
2 FK–(2 grey and 2 green ends)	9 FK–red
4 FK–each of red, grey, and green	12 FK–grey
2 RC–red	14 FK–green

Finish sinnets with a Gathering Knot and trim ends.

Repeat directions for opposite side, working from right to middle.

cascade

216 mm × 1,036 mm (8½ in. × 47 in.)

The combination of two yarns of completely different weights and qualities, and the excitement generated by the interplay between such a combination, provide the outstanding characteristics of this wall hanging. An effect which is a sharp departure from what one usually expects to find in Macramé work is also created by the use of these yarns; for even though the knotting pattern is very obvious, one is more conscious of the yarns used. Therefore, this hanging serves to illustrate the effect that yarns can have in a finished piece.

The yarns used were linen thread and heavy unspun wool called roving. To begin the piece, the wool roving was mounted onto a hardwood bar with the Reversed Cording. A row of Vertical Cording served to introduce the linen thread, which was used double throughout. One row of Flat Knots was then made with the roving, and additional linen was put on with a row of Vertical Cording. Another row of Flat Knots was made, and new ends of linen, using the Reversed Cording, were added between the second and third Flat Knots.

More linen was added on a row of Horizontal Cording, using the Reversed Cording. From here on bobbles were made and the wool and linen areas appear to be independent of each other.

Flat Knots were worked with the linen, using the roving as the core ends. Additional sections of linen were knotted, and then sections of roving, ending with the linen worked over the roving.

KNOTTING PATTERN

In the detail photograph, the section of the wall-hanging which follows is shown with certain areas designated as **A, B,** and **C** in order that you may see more clearly how the knots progressed.

Section **A** shows the definite interplay that was worked between the two areas of linen and roving. Also in this section, the Flat Knots can be seen tied in two different directions, the second being the reverse of the first.

Section **B** illustrates an example of Flat Knots being made with the linen over the roving to give a wrapping effect.

Section **C** shows Flat Knot areas of linen worked independently of the wool. The wool areas are knotted behind the linen. The linen and wool are worked together again as the piece progresses.

The ending of the piece was made with a row of Horizontal Cording, a row of Vertical Cording in roving, a row of Vertical Cording in linen, then a row of Flat Knots in roving, followed by a row of Vertical Cording in linen.

For a fringe effect, the roving was made into sinnets of Flat Knots. The linen was used to tie the Flat Knots with the roving as the core ends.

Enlarged detail of centre section

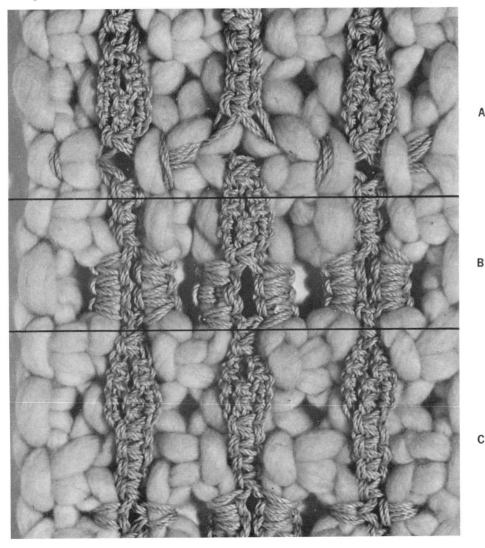

A

B

C

nightbird

140 mm × 914 mm (5½ in. × 36 in.)
Collection of Paul Hodges Allen, Jr

The versatility of the Horizontal Cording is here again demonstrated by still another distinctive pattern obtained by using one of its variations. The most important and interesting section of this wall hanging is another departure from the knotted patterns of the other hangings that have been presented thus far. A scallop-shaped design was accomplished by using the Cording in angling and alternating patterns. Still another design feature of this piece is the way in which the wooden beads were used to accentuate triangular patterns. Since the design was such an intricate one, only one colour was used, causing the beads that are of a brighter value to stand out distinctly.

The materials used were soft thread and wooden beads. This type of thread is not recommended for the beginning knotter since it frays easily, but, when handled with care, it gives a wonderful look to the finished piece that would not be obtainable with a plied yarn.

A 6 heading (see page 24) was made and then mounted onto a holding cord with a row of Horizontal Cordings. The ends were then attached to a dowel, using the Horizontal Cording. Next another row of Horizontal Cording was mounted onto a holding cord, followed by two rows of Flat Knots alternating. At either edge, picots were made during the tying in of rows of Reversed Cording. The area in the centre was formed into a triangular shape by the use of Flat Knots alternating. This shape was emphasized by putting in a border of wooden beads.

To complete this first section, triple and quadruple Flat Knot sinnets were made. They were all tied together by rows of Diagonal Cording which were then underlined with a row of beads. Then another, larger, triangular-shaped area was made, again using the Flat Knot.

The unique pattern of this piece was now worked. In this, Cording angled were tied in and were alternated, so that some were horizontal and others were vertical, often both in the same row. This resulted in the scallop-shaped design mentioned above.

The next area consists of Double Flat Knots alternating. The beads were incorporated into the knotting to form a triangle. The result is in part illusionary since the beads are used in just the top and bottom areas.

The ending began with two rows of Horizontal Cording. A row of Double Flat Knots was made and then a straight row of beads was put on. A row of Double Flat Knots followed, with three rows of Horizontal Cording. Sinnets were made of three Double Flat Knots each. The ends were allowed to hang long and free and were interspersed at intervals with beads and then trimmed off neatly to finish.

Top section of wall-hanging. A row of No. 6 Heading (page 24) was mounted onto a holding cord. Ends were then knotted onto a dowel.

gazebo

965 mm × 610 mm (38 in. × 24 in.)

The hanging here is not a wall-hanging but a circular three-dimensional suspended form. It was chosen to end the section on wall-hangings in order to demonstrate once again the enormous scope of this craft. There is a sculptural quality to this piece which is due in part to its shape and in part to the use of basically simple knots in elaborate patterns. Also, since it is free-hanging, the added quality of motion adds a new interest.

Two different thicknesses of thread in light, neutral colours were used because of the intricate knotting patterns. Small white wooden beads were chosen to harmonize with the design.

The starting ends were bound together at the top, and the knotting was begun from that point (this is a departure from conventional methods). A holding cord and a length of fine wire were coupled together and the beads were knotted on. The rigidity of the wire and the beads combined to form the beginning of the circular shape. As the knotting progressed, additional ends of thread were put on so that the piece

could continue to grow in width. Beads and wire were added throughout this top area to help with the development of the shape.

A number of different knots were used in this section. Bobbles were added at the top and ended in Flat Knot areas. These were secured by two rows of Horizontal Cording. More areas of knots followed, using Cordings and Flat Knots alternating. Beads continued to be added onto the rows of Horizontal Cording which in turn were separated by Flat Knots. A group of Flat Knots using multi-ends were put on, followed by an area of Half Knot sinnets worked with right and left twists. This entire section can be seen in the detail photograph at lower left on the facing page.

This area was then pulled together with two rows of Horizontal Cording, completing the domelike top of the piece. For the next two areas the piece was designed to narrow; therefore beads and wire were not added.

Within these areas the knotting pattern began with Reversed Cording and Flat Knots, followed by two rows of Horizontal Cording, which ended the first section. The second area was worked in alternate rows of Flat Knots using eight ends. These sections are shown in the detail photograph at lower right on the facing page.

With the completion of the narrowed section, more beads and wire were added onto rows of Horizontal Cording, to maintain the circular shaping and to enable the piece to grow in width. This wider area was patterned after the top domelike section.

The ending of the piece was done by making Flat Knot sinnets, multi-end Flat Knots, and additional Flat Knot sinnets. The ends were then left to hang free with beads added at intervals.

(*Facing page, left*) Detail of domelike top section. Note Flat Knot sinnets and Half Knot twisting left-right, right-left. Note also arrangement of wooden beads

(*Facing page, right*) Detail of centre narrowed section. Note alternating Flat Knot sinnets and alternate rows of Flat Knots using eight ends. These areas are separated by two rows of Horizontal Cording

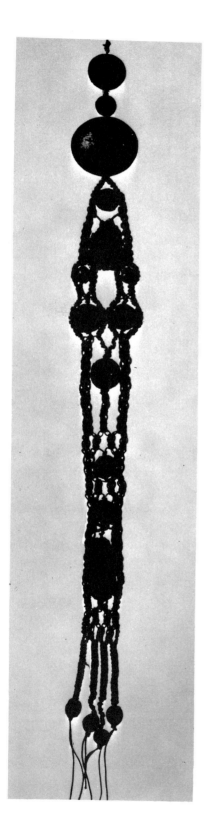

Index

Bibliography

Anchor Manual of Needlework, Batsford, London, 1966.

Ashley, Clifford W., *The Ashley Book of Knots*, Doubleday & Co., Garden City, N.Y., 1944.

De Dillmont, Thérèse, *Encyclopedia of Needlework*, Mulhouse, Alsace, France (no date).

De Dillmont, Thérèse, *Le Macramé*, Mulhouse, Alsace, France (no date).

Groves, Sylvia, *The History of Needlework Tools and Accessories*, Country Life, Ltd., London, 1966.

Harvey, Virginia I., *Macramé, The Art of Creative Knotting*, Van Nostrand Reinhold Co., New York, N.Y., 1967.

Schmid-Burkson, *Fun with Macramé*, Batsford, London, 1972.

Short, Eirian, *Introducing Macramé*, Batsford, London, 1970.

Sylvia's Book of Macramé Lace (c 1882–1885).

Suppliers

Stationers, garden suppliers, hardware stores, yachting and marine suppliers, all sell a variety of strings and ropes which are suitable for Macramé work. Needlecraft and sewing departments of large stores stock threads of all kinds.

General Enquiries,
Leisurecraft Centre,
Search Press Ltd.,
2-10 Jerdan Place,
London, SW6 5PT

Arthur Beale
194 Shaftesbury Avenue
London WC2
will sell over the counter to the general public and will sell small quantities.

Arts and Crafts
10 Byram Street
Huddersfield HD1 LDA
sell *Novacord* matt finish in snowflake, straw and olive and *Novacord* lustre finish in cream, candy floss, brown, café au lait, burnt coffee, bottle, navy, pearl white, red and black.

British Twines Limited
East Ardsley, Wakefield
Yorkshire WF3 2BN
will dye strings to specification for schools and colleges who order in quantity.

Dryad Limited
Northgates
Leicester LE1 4OR
sell fine natural Macramé twine in half-pound balls but will only accept orders by post to the minimum value of £2.

McCulloch and Wallis Limited
25–26 Dering Street
London W1
sell piping cord in boxes containing 23 m (25 *yards*) of the thickest cord to 274 m (300 *yards*) of the finest: bought this way, piping cord works out very economically.

The Needlewoman Shop
146–148 Regent Street
London W1
sell 'Needlewoman' polished twine prepared specially for this firm; available in natural, red, blue, green, yellow, brown and purple.
Strutts Glacé in black, white and unbleached.
Strutts Super Glace Gimp in black, white, cream, light écru, dark écru and brown.
Strutts Super Soft Gimp in red, yellow, light blue, royal blue, green and olive.
Strutts 3-ply Filler Cord, unbleached and in yellow, blue, red and pink.
Novacord matt finish in white, straw and olive.
Novacord lustre finish in cream, peach, pink, café au lait, brown, bottle green, navy, white, red and black.

Wool roving is available from weavers' suppliers.

The Rope Shop
26 High Street
Emsworth
Hants

Also available in this series
Crochet Emily Wildman
Candlemaking Mary Carey
Jewellery Thomas Gentille
Pottery Jolyon Hofsted
Framing Eamon Toscano
Macramé Mary Walker Phillips
Rugmaking Nell Znamierowski
Weaving Nell Znamierowski
Filography Douglas K. Dix
Creative Patchwork June Field
Country Crafts Valerie Janitch
Appliqué Evangeline Shears and Diantha Fielding
Soft Toys Mabs Tyler
More Soft Toys Mabs Tyler
The Art of Dried and Pressed Flowers Pamela Westland and Paula Critchley
The Art of Shellcraft Paula Critchley
Needlework
Creative Patchwork